A Concise Introduction to Microsoft for Windows

ALSO AVAILABLE

A Concise Introduction to Microsoft Works for Windows

by
P.R.M. Oliver
and
N. Kantaris

BERNARD BABANI (publishing) LTD.
THE GRAMPIANS
SHEPHERDS BUSH ROAD
LONDON W6 7NF
ENGLAND

PLEASE NOTE

© 1993 and 1995 BERNARD BABANI (publishing) LTD

First Published - November 1993
Revised Edition - January 1995

British Library Cataloguing in Publication Data:

Oliver P.R.M.
   Concise Introduction to Microsoft WORKS for Windows.
   I. Title II. Kantaris N.
   005.369

   ISBN 0 85934 343 X

Printed and Bound in Great Britain by Cox & Wyman Ltd, Reading

ABOUT THIS BOOK

This Concise Introduction to Microsoft Works for Windows was written to help the beginner, and has been fully revised using Version 3.0a of the software. The material in the book is presented on the 'what you need to know first, appears first' basis. However the underlying structure is such that you don't have to start at the beginning and go right through to the end. The more experienced user can start from any section, as the sections have been designed to be self contained. The book does not, however, describe the workings of Microsoft Windows, or of MS-DOS, or how to set up your computer hardware. If you need to know more about these, then may we suggest that you also refer to the books *A Concise User's Guide to Windows 3.1* (BP325), *A Concise User's Guide to MS-DOS 5* (BP318), or *MS-DOS 6 Explained* (BP341), which are also published by BERNARD BABANI (publishing) Ltd.

Microsoft Works for Windows is a powerful integrated package containing four major types of applications; word processing with drawing, spreadsheet with graphing, database management with reporting and communications. The last of these applications, however, has not been covered in any depth in this book.

The program is operated by selecting commands from menus, from the keyboard, or by clicking Toolbar icons with a mouse. Each method of accessing the package is discussed fully and a complete listing of keyboard shortcuts is included in an Appendix. Using a mouse is not absolutely mandatory, but we cannot imagine many people using Windows without one, and its use certainly increases both productivity and fun.

The power and versatility of Works for Windows is evident in its integration which allows data from any module to be quickly and easily transferred into any of the other modules. The package is a powerful one, offering many commands, and functions. We found the word processor to be almost as powerful as many of the 'stand alone' packages available today. The missing features are the least used anyway.

Microsoft have gone to town with this version of Works regarding the number and quality of both Templates and

WorksWizards supplied with the program. We have not spent much time describing either for two good reasons:

1. They are very user friendly and almost anyone should be able to work through them without too many problems.

2. We feel strongly that you will become more proficient with the Works for Windows program, as a whole, if you build your own applications.

If you want to start off using the 'tailor made' files and documents, have a look through Chapter 9, before getting too much further in the book.

This Concise book is intended as a supplement to the documentation and on-line Help material, that comes with the package. It will provide the new user with a set of examples that will help with the learning of the most commonly used features of the package, and also help provide the confidence needed to tackle some of the more advanced features later.

ABOUT THE AUTHORS

Phil Oliver graduated in Mining Engineering at Camborne School of Mines in 1967 and since then has specialised in most aspects of surface mining technology, with a particular emphasis on computer related techniques. He has worked in Guyana, Canada, several Middle Eastern countries, South Africa and the United Kingdom, on such diverse projects as: the planning and management of bauxite, iron, gold and coal mines; rock excavation contracting in the UK; international mining equipment sales and technical back up and international mine consulting for a major mining house in South Africa. In 1988 he took up a lecturing position at Camborne School of Mines (part of Exeter University) in Surface Mining and Management.

Noel Kantaris graduated in Electrical Engineering at Bristol University and after spending three years in the Electronics Industry in London, took up a Tutorship in Physics at the University of Queensland. Research interests in Ionospheric Physics, led to the degrees of M.E. in Electronics and Ph.D. in Physics. On return to the UK, he took up a Post-Doctoral Research Fellowship in Radio Physics at the University of Leicester, and then in 1973 a lecturing position in Engineering at the Camborne School of Mines, Cornwall, (part of Exeter University), where since 1978 he has also assumed the responsibility for the Computing Department.

If you would like to purchase a floppy disc containing all the files/programs which appear in this, or any other listed book(s) by the same author(s), then fill-in the form at the back of the book and send it to P. R. M. Oliver at the address stipulated.

TRADEMARKS

ACKNOWLEDGEMENTS

We would like to thank the staff of both Microsoft Corporation in the United Kingdom and Text 100 Limited for providing the software programs on which this work was based. We would also like to thank colleagues at both the Camborne School of Mines and Exeter University for the helpful tips and suggestions which assisted us in the writing of this book.

CONTENTS

1. PACKAGE OVERVIEW 1

Installing Works 1

Starting Works 3
    The Welcome Screen 4
    The Startup Screen 4
    The Main Menu 5
    The Main Menu Options 7
    Help Screens 7
    Dialogue Boxes 8
    The Works Screen 10
Cue Cards 13
Manipulating Windows 13
    Changing the Active Window 15
    Closing a Window 15
    Moving Windows and Dialogue Boxes 15
    Sizing a Window 16
    Minimising and Maximising Windows 16
    Splitting a Window 17
    Viewing all Windows 18
Managing Files 18
    Saving a File 18
    Retrieving a File 20
Using the Tutorials 21
Exiting Works 21
The Windows Control Panel 22

2. THE WORKS WORD PROCESSOR 23

Word Processor Basics 23
    The Word Processor Screen 24
    Entering Text 27
    Moving Around a Document 27
Document Editing 29
    Selecting Text 29
    Copying Blocks of Text 31
    Moving Blocks of Text 31
    Drag and Drop Editing 31
    Replacing Blocks of Text 32
    Deleting Blocks of Text 32

The UNDO Command 33
Page Breaks 33
Document Navigation 34
Viewing Word Processor Documents 35
Normal View 35
Page Layout View 35
Draft View 35
Print Preview 35
The Zoom Command 35
Character Enhancement 36
Fonts 38

3. ADVANCED WP FEATURES 41
Paragraph Formatting 41
Indenting Text 42
Hanging Indents 43
Indenting with the Ruler 44
Paragraph Borders 44
Printing Documents 45
Printing from a File 47
Page Setup 48
Print Preview 49
Text Enhancement 50
Tab Settings 50
Headers and Footers 51
Footnotes 54
Endnotes 55
Searching for and Replacing Text 55
Using the Spellchecker 57
Using the Thesaurus 58
Word Count 59
Adding a Note to Your Document 59
Adding a WordArt to Your Document 61
Adding a Drawing to Your Document 62

4. MICROSOFT DRAW 63
The Drawing Tool 63
Importing a Picture 64
Using the Draw Toolbar 65
Draw Menu Commands 66
Creating a Drawing 67

Editing a Drawing 68
Using Layered Drawings 68
Using Line and Fill 68

5. THE WORKS SPREADSHEET 69
Worksheet Navigation 70
The GOTO Command 71
Entering Information 71
Changing Text Alignment and Fonts 73
Changing the Column Width 74
Saving a Worksheet 75
Exiting Works for Windows 77
Filling in a Worksheet 77
Retrieving a Worksheet 77
Formatting Entries 77
Entering Text, Numbers and Formulae 78
Using Functions 79
The Autosum Function 80
Copying Cell Contents 80
Erasing Cell Contents 81
Quick Key Combinations 82
Printing a Worksheet 83
Setting a Print Area 84

6. WORKSHEET SKILLS & GRAPHS 85
The Spreadsheet Toolbar 85
Controlling Cell Contents 87
Inserting Rows & Columns 87
Freezing Titles 88
Non-Contiguous Address Range 90
Relative and Absolute Cell Addresses 90
Moving Cell Contents 92
Some New Features 92
Alignment 92
Automatic Column Widths 92
Inserting Functions 93
The UNDO Command 93
Automatic Cell Fill 93
Cell Formatting Options 93
Adding Spreadsheet Charts 94
Preparing for a Bar Chart 96

The Paste Special Command 97
The Chart Editor 98
Saving Charts 100
Customising a Chart 101
Drawing a Multiple Bar Chart 101
Chart Titles, Fonts & Sizes 102
Printing a Chart 103
Drawing a Pie Chart 104
Mixing Chart Types 105

7. THE DATABASE TOOL **107**
Creating a Database 108
Database Screens 108
Creating a Form 110
Form Editing 112
Hiding a Field Name 113
Entering Data in a Form 113
Using Formulae in a Field 114
Formatting Field Cells 115
Locking Fields 115
Sorting a Database 116
Date Arithmetic 116
The IF Function 118
Searching a Database 120
Database Query 120
The Database Toolbar 122

8. DATABASE APPLICATIONS **123**
Printing from a Database 123
Creating a Report 124
Naming a Report 128
Defining a Report 128
Adding a Report Title 129
Adding Page Titles 130
Using Formulae in a Cell 130
Sorting a Report 131
Completing the Report Definition 132
Applying a Query 133
Printing a Report 133
Form Letters 134
Printing Form Letters 136

9. OTHER PROGRAM FEATURES **137**
The Communications Tool 137
WorksWizards 137
Templates 139
    Sample Files 141

APPENDIX A - FUNCTIONS **143**
Types of Functions 144
    Mathematical Functions 144
    Logical Functions 145
    Financial Functions 145
    Statistical Functions 147
    Text Functions 147
    Date and Time Functions 149
    Special Functions 149

APPENDIX B - QUICK KEY COMBINATIONS .. **151**
Navigation Keys 151
    Moving Between Windows 151
    Moving in a Dialogue Box 151
    Moving in a Document 151
    Moving in a Spreadsheet 152
    Moving in a Database or Report 152
Highlighting Keys 153
    Highlighting in the Word Processor 153
    Highlighting in the Spreadsheet 154
    Highlighting in the Database 155
Editing Keys 155
    Changing Document Information 155
    Changing Appearance of Text or Cells 156
    Inserting Information 156
    Formatting Paragraphs 156
    Working in the Formula Bar 157
    Choosing Menus and Commands 157
INDEX **159**

1. PACKAGE OVERVIEW

Microsoft Works for Windows is an easy to use, integrated package, which incorporates three main modules; word processing, spreadsheet with chart graphics, and database, all of which are downward compatible with earlier DOS versions. Microsoft Draw is included, which allows you to create or modify pictures in the word processor, and if you have a modem, the communications features may also be of interest to you. The package, as its name would suggest, operates inside the graphic interface provided by Microsoft Windows. It comes with full documentation and with WorksWizards. Do not let the name WorksWizards put you off, they simplify several common procedures by stepping you through semi-automated routines.

Installing Works

Microsoft Works for Windows 3.0 can be installed on an IBM compatible PC with at least an 80386 processor and 2MB of RAM, that has a working copy of Microsoft Windows Version 3.1, or later already installed. It needs about 14MB of hard disc space for a full installation. If necessary you could reduce this considerably, in the future, by dispensing with the tutorial and example files. The procedure takes about half an hour and is very easy, involving transferring the working files from the four 3.5 inch floppy system discs to your hard disc and uncompressing them.

To carry out the installation, start Windows in the usual way and insert the Works Setup disc (No. 1) in your drive A:. From the Windows Program Manager screen, activate the **File** menu, by clicking your mouse on **File**, click on **Run** and type

```
A:setup
```

in the **Command Line** box that is opened. Pressing the <Enter> key will produce an opening Welcome Screen with copyright messages and options to **Exit Setup**, **Help** or **OK** to continue. Click on the **Help** button, or press the 'H' key and read the help information (you can action most commands in two ways, either by clicking with the left mouse button, or by pressing the highlighted letter key. Throughout this book the highlighted letter will be shown underlined).

If you are installing from the system discs for the first time, you will be asked for details of your name and company. This information is stored on the first Setup disc and a further installation from the same discs will produce the following fairly strong copyright warning message.

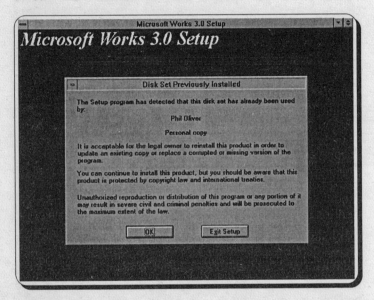

Select **OK** and study the registration details on the next screen. Press **OK** again and either accept C:\MSWORKS as the location directory, or use the **Change Directory** option. **OK** again will give the choice of an automatic, Laptop or manual installation. If you are at all in doubt here, choose the default and let Setup select the best options for your system. We will assume you use the **Complete Installation** but if there is not enough space on your hard disc drive you should use one of the other options.

Accept the Windows Program Group offered by pressing **Continue** and the file copying procedure will start with the bottom window frame keeping you informed about what is happening. When required, you will be asked to place the next disc into the A: drive; a total of four in all. At least the series of information screens help to relieve the boredom!

When the fairly painless operation is complete you should see the Restart Windows box shown here.

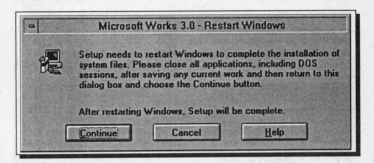

You have little option here but to press **Continue** to let Works complete the installation and restart the Windows program for you.

Hopefully you should have a successful installation and when Windows restarts it should display a newly opened Program Group with three icons in, as shown here.

The Microsoft Works Setup icon is used to reactivate the Setup program if you need to make any changes. The Works Troublshooting icon opens an information file for you to read containing late-breaking information about Microsoft Works 3.0 for Windows. In our case it was Version 3.0a.

Starting Works

It is usual to start the program from the Windows Program Manager, by double clicking on the Microsoft Works icon shown above, which as we saw, was placed by the initial installation procedure.

The Welcome Screen:

When the program is started for the first time the following Welcome box is displayed.

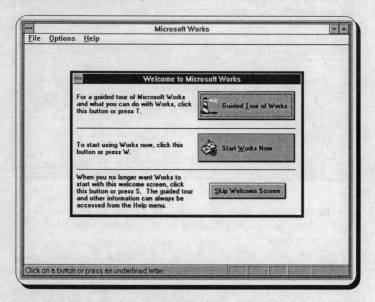

You have 3 buttons to choose from. We suggest you first press the 'S' key to **Skip Welcome Screen** (or click on it with the mouse). Otherwise you will get this screen every time you start up the program. Now might be a good time to take a **Guided Tour of Works**, or if you prefer, click the middle button, or press 'W', to start Works for the first time.

The Startup Screen:

The Startup box, as shown at the top of the next page, will be opened. This is the normal opening screen of Works for Windows. Initially it may seem a little daunting, but you will soon get to know and love it.

Initially the **New & Recent Documents** option is active and the **Word Processor** button has a dotted square box around its icon, indicating that this is the default option, which will be activated if the <Enter> key is pressed. Pressing the <Tab> key will move this 'default marker' from button to

4

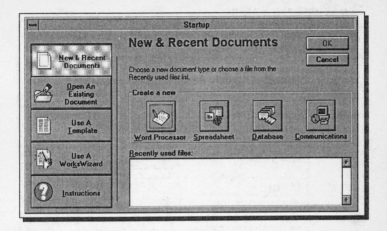

button. It is much easier, though, to click on it with the mouse. These buttons allow you to open a new file in one of Work's 4 tools.

A list of your most **Recently used files** (if any!) is displayed under these buttons. Double clicking on one of the listed files will rapidly open it in the relevant Works tool.

The **Open an Existing Document** option is used for those not recently listed. You select the file in the Windows Open dialogue box and it is opened in the relevant Works tool.

The **Use a Template** and the **Use a WorksWizard** options offer you a choice of semi-automated procedures to carry out. **Instructions** describes the operation of the Startup box in more detail.

We suggest you experiment with these options later, but at the moment simply press the <Esc> key, or select **Cancel**, to obtain the basic, or common, Works menu screen, shown on the next page.

The main Works menu, as shown here, has the item 'File' in the menu highlighted, with its pull-down sub-menu displayed underneath. The pull-down sub-menus associated with the other two items of the main menu can be seen by pressing the right arrow key. Pressing the <Esc> key clears the sub-menus.

▬		Microsoft Works	▾	▴

File   Tools   Help

| Create New File... |
| Open Existing File... |
| WorksWizards... |
| Templates... |
| Close |
| Save   Ctrl+S |
| Save As... |
| Save Workspace |
| Exit Works |

The Main Menu:

To activate the main menu, either press the <Alt> key, which causes the first item of the menu (in this case **File**) to be highlighted, then use the right and left arrow keys to highlight any of the items in the main menu; or use the mouse to point to an item. Pressing either the <Enter> key, or the left mouse button, reveals the pull-down sub-menu of the highlighted menu item.

Main menu options can also be activated directly by pressing the <Alt> key followed by the underlined letter of the required option. Thus pressing <Alt+o>, causes the one item pull-down sub-menu of **Tools** to be displayed. You can use the up and down arrow keys to move the highlighted bar up and down a sub-menu, or the right and left arrow keys to move along the options of the main menu. As each option is highlighted, a short description of the function of the relevant option or command appears in the status line at the bottom of the screen. Pressing the <Enter> key selects the highlighted option, or executes the highlighted command. Pressing the <Esc> key closes the menu system and returns you to the main menu.

Selection of a sub-menu item can also be achieved by either typing the underlined letter of the required command, or using the mouse to point to the required command and pressing the left mouse button.

If you use a mouse, there is a quick way of selecting an item from the main menu by pointing to it and pressing the left mouse button; then, with the button depressed, drag the mouse down the revealed sub-menu which highlights each sub-menu item in turn. Once the required item has been highlighted, release the mouse button to select it.

The Main Menu Options:
Each item of the main menu offers the following options:

<u>F</u>ile   Produces a pull-down menu, as shown, of mainly file related tasks, such as creating a new file, opening an existing file from disc and displaying it on screen, closing a file, saving a file to disc, saving workspace and exiting Works. Options are also included to handle WorksWizards and Templates

T<u>o</u>ols   This menu is most unusual in that it only has one item that defines the option settings for Works.

<u>H</u>elp   Activates the help window, gives a package overview, displays the help contents, offers advice on how to use either help, or the Works package, and gives access to Cue Cards and the Works tutorial.

Note that some sub-menu options, such as the **<u>S</u>ave**, **Save <u>A</u>s** and **<u>C</u>lose** options of the **<u>F</u>ile** menu, appear in fainter grey text than, say, the **<u>O</u>pen Existing File** option. This means that you cannot access them. In this particular instance you cannot save work you have not created yet, or close a file that has not been opened.

Help Screens:
Works has context-sensitive help screens which explain the use of the items in the various menus, or commands, you are attempting to use. Thus, to obtain help information on the use of any of the options offered under **<u>F</u>ile**, as shown on the facing page, first choose the **<u>F</u>ile** command, then use the down arrow key to highlight the desired task from the pull-down sub-menu, and then press the **F1** function key.

You can re-size, move, tile, or cascade the Help window and the current document so that you can keep both of them

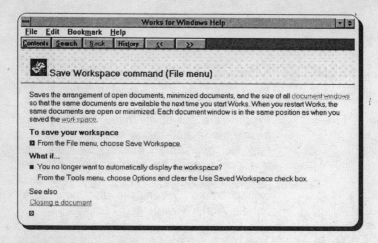

Save Workspace command (File menu)

Saves the arrangement of open documents, minimized documents, and the size of all document windows so that the same documents are available the next time you start Works. When you restart Works, the same documents are open or minimized. Each document window is in the same position as when you saved the workspace.

To save your workspace

▣ From the File menu, choose Save Workspace.

What if...

■ You no longer want to automatically display the workspace?
From the Tools menu, choose Options and clear the Use Saved Workspace check box.

See also

Closing a document
▣

displayed and you can even copy and edit text from the Help windows into a document.

Spend some time exploring the Help system. Most of the Works manual contents are in it; you just have to find them. A quick way to start would be to select **Works overview**, read each screen of information and then click the >> button to move to the next page. Many Help topics contain cross-references to other related Help topics, which display in green. These are often known as 'hypertext' links, and clicking the hand mouse pointer on them displays their content. You can 'jump around' the Help system in this way.

Dialogue Boxes:

Three periods after a sub-menu option or command, means that a dialogue box will open when the option or command is selected. A dialogue box is used for the insertion of additional information, such as the name of a file under which to save your current work.

To illustrate how they work, select the **Tools**, **Options**, command which will display the dialogue box shown at the top of the next page.

When a dialogue box opens, the <Tab> and <Shift+Tab> keys can be used to move the cursor from one field to another in a clockwise or anti-clockwise direction, respectively. Once in the selected field, the up and down

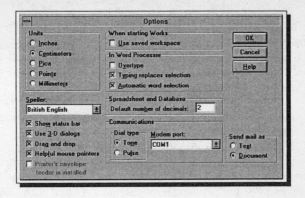

arrow keys can be used to select different options. The
<Enter> key is only used to indicate that the options within
the various fields within the dialogue box are specified
correctly.

Every dialogue box contains one field which is enclosed in
a dotted rectangle (**Centimeters**, in the above example).
This field indicates the action that Works will take if the
<Enter> key is pressed. Pressing the <Esc> key, aborts the
dialogue box and menu option and returns you to the main
menu.

With a mouse, to select any item within any field, simply
point to it and click the left mouse button. To confirm your
selections, click on the **OK** button. Clicking the **Cancel**
button, aborts the dialogue box and menu option and returns
you to the main menu.

There are five types of field boxes in a dialogue box; 'List',
'Option', 'Check', 'Text' and 'Command buttons'. Referring to
the previous display **Speller** is an example of a 'List' box. An
item can be selected either by using the up and down arrow
keys, or by pointing and clicking at it with the mouse. If there
are more options than fit the box, either use the down arrow
key, or click the down scroll arrow, on the right of the 'List'
box, to see the next available option.

Units is an example of an 'Option' box. A dot enclosed in a
round hole against an option signifies that the particular
option is selected. Only one option can be selected at a time.
To change the selected option, either press the underlined

9

letter of the option you want to select, or point to it with the mouse and click.

In a 'Check' box the options can either be 'on' (marked with an 'X' in a square hole) or 'off'. You can select more than one option in a check box, as shown.

A 'Text' box, is a box into which you can either type new information or change what is there by editing it. (**Default number of decimals** in our example).

You press a 'Command button' to execute a certain command, such as the **OK** button in the **Options** display. Command buttons in Works for Windows are rectangular and a preselected button is shown with a dotted box. Most dialogue boxes have the three command buttons; **OK**, **Help** and **Cancel**. To select a command button, either use the <Tab> key to highlight it and press <Enter>, or point to it with the mouse and click.

The Works Screen:

It is perhaps worth spending some time looking at the various parts that make up the Works for Windows screen. To illustrate our discussion, use the **File, Create New File** command if you are within Works. If not, start the program and select **Spreadsheet** from the Startup box by pressing 'S', or by clicking its button with your mouse. Note that the screen window produced now displays a new list of menu names at the top, a Toolbar with a series of pictorial icons below, a window title (SHEET1, in this case) below this, an empty worksheet with numbered rows and lettered columns, and a Cue Cards window which offers on-line help. This feature is turned off in the example shown, for clarity.

Works follows the usual Microsoft Windows conventions and if you are familiar with these you can skip through this section. Otherwise a few minutes might be well spent here.

The window, as shown on the facing page, takes up the full screen area available. If you click on the application restore button, the top one of the two restore buttons at the top right of the screen, you can make Works show in a smaller window. This can be useful when you are running several applications at the same time and you want to transfer between them with the mouse. Although multiple worksheet, database and document files can be displayed

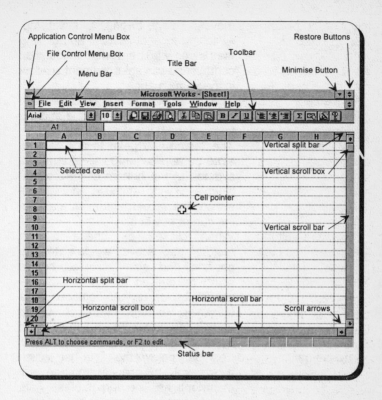

simultaneously in their own windows, you can only enter data into the active window (highlighted at the top). Title bars of non active windows appear a lighter shade than that of the active one.

The Works for Windows screen is divided into several areas which have the following functions. These are described from the top of the screen down, working from left to right.

Area	Function
Control boxes	Clicking on the top control menu box, which is located in the upper left corner of the window, displays the pull-down Control menu which can be used to control the program window. It includes commands for re-sizing,

moving, maximising, minimising, switching to another task and closing the window. The lower menu box controls the current document window in the same manner.

Title bar	The bar at the top of a window which displays the application name and the name of the current document.
Minimise box	The button you point to and click to store an application as an icon (small symbol) at the bottom of the screen. Double clicking on such an icon will restore the screen and even maintain the cursor position.
Restore buttons	When clicked on, these buttons restore the active window to the position and size occupied before being maximised or minimised. The restore button is then replaced by a Maximise button, with a single up-pointing arrow, which can be used to set the window to its former size.
Menu bar	The bar below the title bar which allows you to choose from several menu options. The names of the main menu commands might be different when using a different tool. To display a sub-menu, click on the name or press <Alt> followed by the underlined letter.
Toolbar	Displays a set of icons for each tool, which can be clicked on to quickly carry out commands or functions.
Scroll bars	The areas on the screen (extreme right and bottom of each window) that contain scroll boxes in vertical and horizontal bars. Clicking on these bars allows you to control the part of a document which is visible on the screen.

| Scroll arrows | The arrowheads at each end of each scroll bar at which you can click to scroll the screen up and down one line, or left and right 10% of the screen, at a time. |
| Status bar | The bottom line of the screen that displays the current program status and information regarding the present process. |

Cue Cards

Cue Cards are a feature new to Works for Windows Version 3.0. They display automatically in a window that sits on top of the opened working windows and give step by step instructions to help with the task currently being carried out. Like other windows, you can move a Cue Card around the screen, or reduce it to an icon with its minimise button, but you cannot change its size.

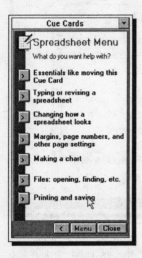

Once you have found your way around the Works program, you will probably find that the Cue Cards get in the way. Simply click the Close button to get rid of them from the screen. If you need them back in the future, use the **Help**, **Cue Cards** menu command.

Manipulating Windows

Works allows the display of multiple sets of data within a given application tool, or several windows encompassing files from different application tools, each within its own window.

At some stage, you will almost certainly need to manipulate these windows, by selecting which is to be the active window, moving them so that you can see all the relevant parts of an application, re-sizing them, or indeed closing unwanted windows once you have finished with them. A short discussion follows on how to manipulate windows so

13

that you can get the best of what Works for Windows can provide.

In order to illustrate our discussion, use the **File, Create New File** command three successive times and choose, in turn, a different tool option from those displayed in the dialogue box. As each selection is made, a new, titled, window is displayed, with new windows being placed on top of any existing ones, as shown below.

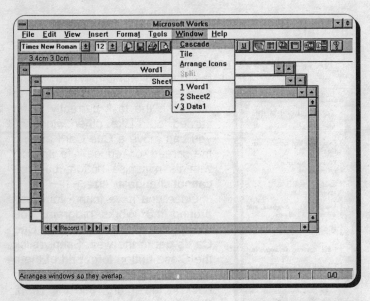

If you create a certain type of window file using the same tool more than once in any work session, this is reflected in the number appearing immediately after the default name of that particular window. You should save your work using different names from these default ones (with each name no more than 8 characters long). The three letter file extensions are added by Works and are always the same for each tool as the ones displayed. Note that the active window has a highlighted title bar, while the non active title bars are white.

The filename extensions of the four application tools are:

Extension	Tool
WPS	Works Word Processor
WKS	Works Spreadsheet
WDB	Works Database
WCM	Works Communications

Changing the Active Window:

You can select the active window, from amongst those displayed on the screen, by pointing to any part of it, and clicking the mouse button, or by selecting the **Window** command of the main menu and selecting the appropriate number of the window you want to make the active one.

Closing a Window:

Works itself, or any tool window (provided it is the active window), can be closed at any time, maybe to save screen space and memory. To close the DATA1 window, make it the active window and either double click on the File Control Menu Box (the large hyphen in the upper-left corner of the window, or press the <Ctrl+F4> keys, or use the **File, Close** command.

If you have made any changes to a file in a window since the last time you saved it, Works will warn you with the appearance of a dialogue box giving you the option to save the file before closing it.

Moving Windows and Dialogue Boxes:

When you have multiple windows or dialogue boxes on the screen, you might want to move a particular one to a different part of the screen. This can be achieved with either the mouse or the keyboard, but not if the window occupies the full screen, for obvious reasons.

To move a window, or a dialogue box, with the mouse, point to the title bar and drag it (press the left button and keep it pressed while moving the mouse) until the shadow border is where you want it to be. Then release the mouse button to fix it into its new position.

To move with the keyboard, press <Alt+Spacebar> to reveal the Application Control Menu, or <Alt+—> to reveal the Document Control menu. Then, press 'M', to select **Move,** which causes a four-headed arrow to appear in the title bar and use the arrow keys to move the shadow border of the window to the required place. Press <Enter> to fix the window to its new position, or <Esc> to cancel the relocation.

Sizing a Window:

You can change the size of a window with either the mouse or the keyboard. To size an active window with the mouse, move the window so that the side you want to change is visible, then move the mouse pointer to the edge of the window or corner, so that it changes to a two-headed arrow, then drag the two-headed arrow in the direction you want that side or corner to move. Continue dragging until the shadow border is the size you require, then release the mouse button.

To size with the keyboard, press either <Alt+Spacebar> or <Alt+—> to reveal the Application Control menu or the Document Control menu, then press 'S' to select **Size**, which causes the four-headed arrow to appear. Now press the arrow key that corresponds to the edge you want to move, or if a corner, press the two arrow keys (one after the other) corresponding to the particular corner, which causes the pointer to change to a two-headed arrow. Press an appropriate arrow key in the direction you want that side or corner to move and continue to do so until the shadow border is the size you require, then press <Enter> to fix the new window size.

Minimising and Maximising Windows:

Works for Windows can be minimised into an icon at the bottom of the screen; you may want to do this if you have another Windows application running and need to change over to it. This can be done either by using the mouse to click at the 'Minimise' button (the downward arrow in the upper-right corner of the window), or by pressing <Alt+Spacebar> or <Alt+—> to reveal the Application Control menu or the Document Control menu, and selecting 'n' for **Minimise**.

To maximise a window so that it fills the entire screen, either click on the 'maximise' button (the upward arrow in the upper-right corner of the window), or press <Alt+Spacebar> or <Alt+−> to display the Application Control menu or the Document Control menu, and select 'x' for **Maximise**.

An application which has been minimised or maximised can be returned to its original size and position on the screen by either double-clicking on its icon to expand it to a window, or clicking on the double-headed button in the upper-right corner of the maximised window to reduce it to its former size. With the keyboard, press <Alt+Spacebar> to display the Application Control menu, or <Alt+−> to display the Document Control menu, and press 'R' for **Restore**.

Splitting a Window:

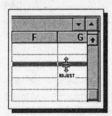

The windows of two Works application tools can be split, so that you can see different parts of your work side by side in the same window. You can split the word window horizontally and the spreadsheet window both horizontally and vertically.

To split a window, move the mouse pointer onto a split bar (the bar either below the maximise arrow, or to the left of the horizontal scroll arrow), drag the new pointer shape to the required position (as shown in our example above), and release the

mouse button. Otherwise you could use the **Window, Split** command, then the arrow keys to move the shadow split lines, as shown alongside, to the required position and press <Enter>.

The figure on the next page shows the word processor window split into two areas and the active spreadsheet window into four areas.

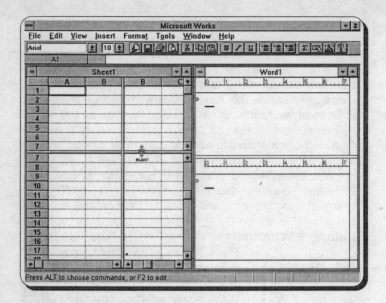

Viewing All Windows:

You can arrange to view all the windows currently on the screen by using the **Window, Tile** command. Works automatically arranges the windows on screen. Three windows are placed full screen height and next to each other, while four are placed with a quarter of the screen each. If you are experimenting with the program as you go, watch how the mouse pointer changes shape, depending on where it is and what it is doing.

Managing Files

Works for Windows allows you to create, save, open, or generally operate on files, by using the **File** command from either the main menu of the package, or from the menu of any of its tools.

Saving a File:

Once a document has been prepared, under any of the tool applications, you can save it by using the **File, Save** command. The first time you use this command with, say, the word processor, Works asks you in a dialogue box for a filename to save under. With this tool, the default filename for the first opened window is WORD1, as shown below. You can type a new name, say, MEMO (without any extension) and press <Enter>, which causes the typed filename to become the new document title. Once a file has been saved, subsequent use of the **File, Save** command, saves the file automatically under the filename, directory and drive, first used to save your work.

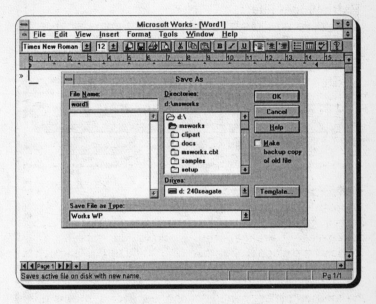

To change the drive or directory from its default, which might be C:\MSWORKS to, say, A:\MSWORKS, open the **Drives** drop down list box, by clicking its arrow, and then click 'a:'. Move to the **Directories** box (press <Alt+D> with the keyboard), use the arrow keys to highlight the required directory from the displayed list and press <Enter>.

If you want to save an already saved file under a different name, then use the **File, Save As** command. Works for Windows again offers you, in the same dialogue box, the original filename which you can change by typing a different name, without an extension (the moment you start typing the new name, the default name vanishes from the display). On pressing <Enter>, the program adds automatically the appropriate extension for you and saves the file.

The **Save File as Type** box allows you to save the file in any of the formats listed. You would select 'Wordperfect 5.1', for instance, if you wanted to use the file later in that package.

Retrieving a File:

To retrieve an already saved document from disc, use the **File, Open Existing File** command. This will bring up the following dialogue box:

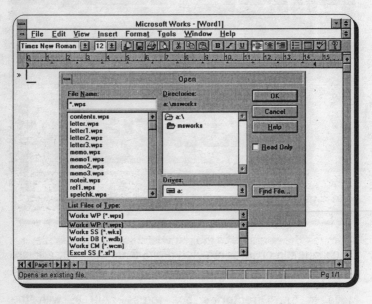

In this case the open directory is A:\MSWORKS and in the **File Name** box the file template name '*.wps' is displayed. This is because 'Works WP (*.wps)' has been selected in the **List Files of Type** box. To select the MEMO.WPS file, you would either click at its name with the mouse pointer, or press <Alt+N> to move into the **File Name** box, press <Tab> to move the highlight down into the file list, highlight the required file and press <Enter>. The mouse method is definitely preferable!

Using the Tutorials

Works comes with a set of comprehensive tutorials which can be accessed from within the package (provided you have installed them on the hard disc) by selecting the **Help, Tutorial** command, or pressing the <Shift+**F1**> keys. The following very colourful display is opened.

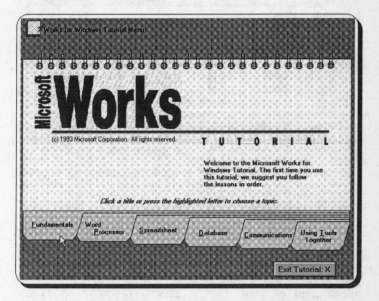

Although the contents of the early tutorials can be simple, it is worth spending some time on them to learn the language and definitions associated with the various Works for Windows applications. We leave it to you to explore further.

Exiting Works

Whenever you are ready to leave the Works for Windows package the procedure is the same whichever tool you are in. You simply use the **File**, **Exit Works** command. If all the open files have been saved, you will be returned immediately to the Windows Program Manager. If not you will be given the option to save them, before they are lost forever.

The Windows Control Panel

The Control Panel provides a quick and easy way to change the hardware and software settings of your system. For the sake of completeness we describe its use at this point.

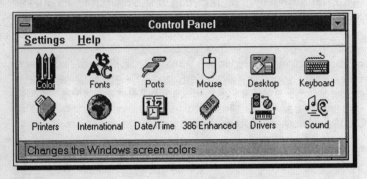

Access to the Control Panel is made by double clicking the Control Panel icon in the **Main** group window of the Program Manager. Selecting this option opens the above window from which the various Control Panel functions can be accessed.

Double-clicking at the Control Panel icons allows you to change the display colours, change the display and printer fonts, specify parameters for any serial ports installed on your system, change the settings of your mouse, change the appearance of your display, specify resource allocations when running in 386 mode, install and configure your printer(s), specify international settings, such as the formatting of numbers and dates, change the keyboard repeat rate, change the date and time of your system, and specify whether Windows should beep when it detects an error.

All of these features control the environment in which Works for Windows (and other Windows application packages) operate and you should become familiar with them.

22

2. THE WORKS WORD PROCESSOR

Works for Windows comes equipped with a word processor almost as powerful as most 'stand alone' versions. It has all the normal editing features, including the ability to insert, delete, erase, search for, replace, drag and drop copy and move characters, lines and whole blocks of text. As you would expect, it also allows you to enhance text and create bold, underlined, italic, strike-through, superscript, subscript and other specially formatted text. Being an integrated package it is easy to embed part of a spreadsheet into a document, carry out a mail merge, or send a document to a distant computer using the communications functions.

Word Processor Basics

To access the word processor select **File, Create New File** from the opening menu bar, as described in the previous chapter. Then select the **Word Processor** button by either pressing the **W** key, or pressing <Enter>, as this is the highlighted option. A screen similar to that shown below will appear, with the file WORD1 opened for you.

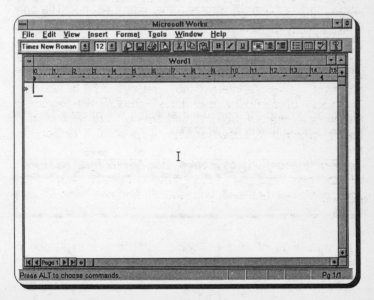

When you save your work later you should rename this, or else the file may be overwritten when WORD1.WPS is next opened automatically and saved again. If you open more than one new file, in the same session, they will be numbered Word1, Word2, and so on.

The Word Processor Screen:

The top line of this screen gives the menu bar, which with the word processor, accesses the following sub menus:

```
File  Edit  View  Insert  Format  Tools  Window  Help
```

As described in the 'Package Overview' these are accessed either with your mouse, or by pressing the <Alt> key followed by the underlined letter.

The Toolbar occupies the second line down. If you use a mouse you will find this a big time saver, once you get in the habit of using it. If you prefer, you can turn it off by activating the **View**, **Toolbar** command. This is a toggle, when the '√' shows the Toolbar will display, otherwise it will not. The only advantage to be gained by not showing it is you gain one screen line.

When you move the mouse pointer over one of the icons a yellow message box showing its function opens up, as shown below.

To use the Toolbar you simply click the mouse on one of the options, and the command selected will affect all text in the document that is highlighted.

The meanings of all the Toolbar options are explained in more detail on the facing page.

Option	Result
`Times New Roman ▼`	Choose a font from available list. Clicking the arrow (↓) will open the list of fonts.
`12 ▼`	Choose from available point sizes. Clicking the arrow (↓) will open the list of sizes.
	Open Start-up box
	Save current document
	Print current document
	Print preview
	Cut to clipboard
	Copy to clipboard
	Paste from clipboard
	Embolden selected text
	Make selected text italic
	Underline selected text
	Left align a paragraph
	Centre align a paragraph
	Right align a paragraph
	Create a bullet list
	Insert a table or range
	Turn spell checker on
	Start On-line Help

Version 3.0 of Works allows you to change the icons on the toolbar from the Customize Works Toolbar box, opened with the **Tools**, **Customize** command.

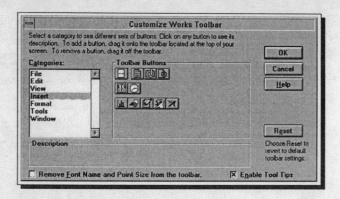

You simply drag any icons you don't want from the toolbar and drag ones you do to the bar, from the Toolbar Buttons section. Press the **Reset** button to abandon your changes.

The 'title bar' of the document window, the next line down when not full screen, shows the name of the opened document. If this bar is dragged with the mouse the window can be moved around the screen.

Below the title bar is the ruler which appears as a scale across the screen. This shows and allows you to change the left and right margin positions and any tab or indent settings active in the paragraph the cursor is in. You change the settings by dragging the markers across the ruler, which can be toggled on and off like the Toolbar, with the **View**, **Ruler** command.

The bottom line of the screen is the status line which gives you useful information on the operation being carried out, or a description of the highlighted command. It also shows the current document page, the total number of pages, and the status of any keys that are currently locked.

The horizontal scroll bar has a new page control feature built into it, as shown here. Mouse clicking on the four arrows moves the insertion point as shown.

To beginning of document
Back one page
Current page number

Forward one page
To end of document

The other scroll bars, boxes and arrows described in the last chapter also surround the work area which makes up the remainder of the screen.

Whenever a Works word processing file is opened three marks always appear at the top left corner of the screen working area:

»   The page mark which identifies the beginning of a page.

| The blinking vertical line is the cursor. Any text typed will be placed at this position.

_   The end mark which identifies the end of a document. This mark cannot be erased from the screen. All text, etc., must be placed above it. The mark can be forced down the screen by pressing <Enter> when the cursor is above it, which inserts blank lines.

Entering Text:

Before going any further enter the memo text shown overleaf, or something else if you prefer, to begin to get the feel of Works word processing.

When a new file is opened it is ready for you to begin typing in text. Any time you want to force a new line, or paragraph, just press <Enter>, otherwise the program will sort out line lengths automatically which is known as word wrap. So, you can just carry on typing a complete paragraph without having to press any keys to move to a new line. If you make a mistake, at this stage, press <BkSp> enough times to erase the mistake and retype it.

Now would be a good time to save the document, as described in the previous chapter, press **File, Save As** and type a new drive, path and filename, as required. For example, change to **A:\MEMO1** to save to a floppy disk in the A: drive. The program will add the WPS extension for you.

Moving Around a Document:

You can move the cursor around a document with the normal direction keys, with the key combinations shown below, or with the **Edit**, **Go To** command (or press **F5**). With the last

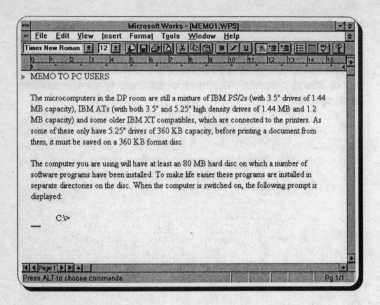

command you can jump to various named 'bookmarks', or to different page numbers, as described later on.

To move	*Press*
Left one character	←
Right one character	→
Up one line	↑
Down one line	↓
Left one word	Ctrl+←
Right one word	Ctrl+→
Up one paragraph	Ctrl+↑
Down one paragraph	Ctrl+↓
To beginning of line	Home
To end of line	End
To beginning of file	Ctrl+Home
To end of file	Ctrl+End
Up one window	Pg Up
Down one window	Pg Dn
To beginning of window	Ctrl+Pg Up
To end of window	Ctrl+Pg Dn

Document Editing

It will not be long when using the word processor before you will need to edit your screen document. This could be to delete unwanted words, to correct a mistake or to add extra text in the document. All these operations are very easy to carry out.

For small deletions, such as letters or words, the easiest method is using the <Del> or <BkSp> keys. With the <Del> key, position the cursor on the first letter to delete and press <Del>; the letter is deleted and the following text moves one space to the left.

With the <BkSp> key, position the cursor immediately to the right of the character to be deleted and press <BkSp>; the cursor moves one space to the left pulling the rest of the line with it and overwriting the character to be deleted.

Word processing is usually carried out in the insert mode. Any characters typed will be inserted at the cursor location and the following text will be pushed to the right, and down, to make room. Pressing the <Ins> key will change you to overstrike mode and the letters 'OVR' will appear on the Status Line. In this mode any text you type will over-write existing text.

To insert blank lines in your text, make sure you are in Insert mode, place the cursor at the beginning of the line where the blank is needed and press <Enter>. The cursor line will move down leaving a blank line. To remove the blank line position the cursor at its left end and press <Del>.

When larger scale editing is needed, such as using the copy, move and erase operations, the text to be altered must be 'selected', or 'highlighted', before the operation can be carried out. These functions are then available when the **Edit** sub-menu is activated, the Toolbar options used, or Drag and Drop is used.

Selecting Text:

The procedure in Works for Windows, before any operation such as formatting or editing can be carried out on text, is first to select the text to be altered. Selected text is highlighted on the screen. This can be carried out in several ways.

Using the keyboard, position the cursor on the first character to be selected and either:

a.   Hold down the <Shift> key while using the direction keys to highlight the required text, then release the <Shift> key, or:

b.   Press the **F8** key and use the direction keys to highlight the required text, or:

c.   Press **F8** TWO times to select a WORD

Press **F8** THREE times to select a SENTENCE

Press **F8** FOUR times to select a PARAGRAPH

Press **F8** FIVE times to select whole DOCUMENT.

With the mouse:

a.   Left click at the beginning of the block and drag the cursor across the block so that whole words of the desired text are highlighted, then release the mouse button.

b.   With the cursor in a word double click the left mouse button to select that word.

c.   Position the cursor in the left window margin and then either click the left button to select the current LINE, or double-click the left button to select the current PARAGRAPH, or hold down the <Ctrl> key and click the left mouse button to select the entire DOCUMENT.

When using the **F8** key method, 'EXT' is displayed on the status line with the message 'Selects range of text' to indicate that extended highlighting of text is taking place. The selection can be collapsed one level at a time by pressing <Shift+F8>.

Try out all these methods and find which ones you are most comfortable with.

Copying Blocks of Text:

Once text has been selected it can be copied to another location in your present document, to another Works document (as long as it is open), to another Works tool, or even to another program working in the Windows environment. As with most of the editing and formatting operations there are several ways of doing this. One is by using the **Edit, Copy** command sequence from the menu, moving the cursor to the start of where you want the copied

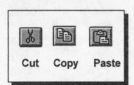

Cut Copy Paste

text, and use the **Edit**, **Paste** command. You can also use toolbar icons, or quick key combinations (details of which are included in Appendix B). Press the Copy icon, or <Ctrl+C>, once the text to be copied has been

selected, and the Paste icon, or <Ctrl+V>, to 'paste' it in the new location. These methods do not require the menu bar to be activated.

To copy the same text again to another location in the document, move the cursor to the new location and Paste it. This operation is called 'pasting' because of the old days (for some of us) with scissors and a glue pot!

When text is copied, or cut, it is actually placed on the Window's 'clipboard' and remains there until replaced by other text.

Moving Blocks of Text:

Selected text can be moved to any location on the same document. To do this, 'cut' it to the clipboard with the **Edit**, **Cut** command (<Ctrl+X>) and then 'paste' it in the new location with the **Edit**, **Paste** command (<Ctrl+V>). The moved text will be placed at the cursor location and will force any existing text to make room for it. This operation can be cancelled before the final key command by simply pressing <Esc>.

Drag and Drop Editing:

Probably the easiest way to copy and move blocks of text in a document is with the new Drag and Drop feature. You have probably noticed that when you move the pointer over a selected block it changes to the DRAG pointer shown. To move the block, drag it with the left mouse button depressed. To copy it, hold down the <Ctrl> key while you drag. The pointer will change to either a MOVE or COPY arrow and a small vertical bar will follow it around the screen, as shown here. Place this bar at the new start position of the text and release the mouse button. The new text will insert itself where placed, even if the overstrike mode is active. Text moved, or copied, in this way is not placed on the clipboard, so multiple operations are not possible.

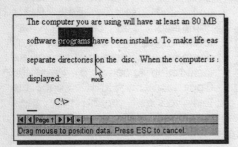

Replacing Blocks of Text:
One block of text can be 'replaced' by another using either the cut or copy process. Obviously if cut is used the text at the original location will be removed, but not if the copy command is used. The process is the same as an ordinary copy or move, except that the block of text to be replaced must be selected before the final 'paste' command is made.

Deleting Blocks of Text:
When text is cut or deleted it is removed from the document. With Works for Windows any selected text can be deleted by pressing the <Del> key. This will not, however, place the deleted text on the Windows clipboard, for possible future use. To do this you must use the **Edit**, **Cut** command, icon, or <Ctrl+X>.

The UNDO Command:

As text is lost with the delete command you should use it with caution, but if you do make a mistake all is not lost as long as you act immediately. The **Edit, Undo** command reverses your most recent editing or formatting command, so you need to use it before carrying out any further operations. This works even after Drag and Drop actions. Immediately after you undo a command or action, the **Undo** command changes to the **Redo** command, which allows you to restore what you've reversed. The quick key sequence for the Undo/Redo command is <Ctrl+Z>.

Page Breaks:

The program automatically inserts a page break in a document when a page of typed text is full. The page break symbol (») tells the printer where to end one page and start printing another. There will be places in most multi-page documents where you will want to force a new page to improve the layout. This is done by inserting a manual page break by pressing **Insert**, **Page Break,** or just using the key combination <Ctrl+Enter>. Works readjusts all the non-manual page breaks for the remainder of the document.

To demonstrate this, retrieve the document previously saved as MEMO1.WPS. Note there is a page marker on the left hand side of line 1, in the margin next to the title line. Press <Ctrl+End> to place the cursor at the end of the document and just above the end of file marker. In this position you will not be able to move down further. Insert a page break as described above (**Insert**, **Page Break**). Your cursor should now be at the start of Page 2, with a line of dots indicating where the manual break was placed, as shown below.

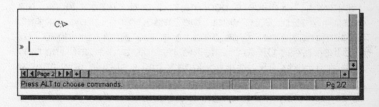

Now press <Enter> repeatedly (or type lots of text) until the status line indicates 'Pg 3/3', or higher. This is just a quick way of adding more pages, albeit empty ones, to the document. Move the cursor up to the page break which was automatically inserted between pages 2 and 3. There is no line of dots. A manual page break can be deleted, but an automatic one cannot, so they appear differently on the screen.

Frustratingly, Works for Windows can take several seconds for the screen to sort out its automatic page breaks, especially with a long document, and it can fall behind you. If this becomes a problem simply use the **Tools**, **Paginate Now** command, or **F9**, to force an immediate repagination of the document on screen.

Document Navigation:

Now we have several 'pages' in a document it is a good time to explore some methods of navigating large documents. You can use the page control buttons on the horizontal scroll bar, but there are also two methods of jumping to specific document locations. Both use the **Edit**, **Go To** command, or **F5** for short. This brings up the dialogue box shown here.

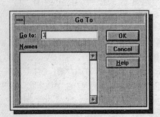

Type **3** in the **Go to** text box, press **OK**, or <Enter>, and the cursor should jump straight to the top of page 3 in the document. This is a quick way of moving to the top of any page.

The other method uses the same box but uses 'bookmarks' which you place at strategic locations in your document. To place a bookmark in a document locate the cursor where you want the mark and press **Insert**, **Bookmark Name**. Type a name in the empty dialogue box and then press **OK** to create the invisible bookmark. The next time you press **F5**, your bookmark name should now appear in the box under **Names.** Highlight this, press **OK**, and the cursor should jump to where the bookmark was placed. In a long document placing bookmarks at the start of each section makes it easy to find your way around.

Viewing Word Processor Documents

Works provides four ways to view your document on the screen. Each view allows you to concentrate on different aspects of your work. Choose the view you want from the **View** menu, except for **File**, **Print Preview**.

Normal View:

This is the default working view. This view shows text and paragraph formatting, line and page breaks, tab and paragraph alignment. Normal view, however, displays only a single column of text.

Page Layout View:

This fully WYSIWYG (what you see is what you get) view displays each page in your document as it will look when printed. Columns, headers, footers and footnotes appear in their correct positions and you can edit them in this view. It is also excellent for working with embedded objects, such as pictures and graphics. Page layout view is often slower than other views, unless you have a fast PC.

Draft View:

Working in draft view can speed up working with large documents as it displays all text in one font and size, and inserted pictures as empty frames. Very much the older DOS word processor view!

Print Preview:

This shows a view of your document to show one page on the screen exactly as it will be printed. You can't edit text or make any changes in print preview.

The Zoom Command:

The Zoom feature allows you to control the amount of the active document that will display on the screen at any time, when you are in Normal or Page Layout modes. The zoom size status of a particular document has no effect on the document when it is printed.

From the **View** menu, choose **Zoom**, and then choose the size you want from the dialogue box as follows:

To display a document	Choose
Four times its normal size	400
Twice its normal size	200
As it will be printed	100
At a reduced size	75
At half the normal size	50

With the **C**ustom option you can specify any magnification factor between 25 and 1000.

Character Enhancement

Another simplistic example will explain the principles of text enhancement. With Works for Windows it is often easier to type your text in first and worry about the document layout later on. Create a new word processing file and type in the letter text shown below.

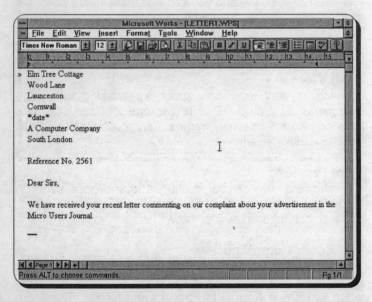

The date formula *date* on line 5 will give the current date when the letter is printed, and is generated with the quick key combination <Ctrl+D>. Alternatively, the current date could have been placed straight into the letter with the <Ctrl+;>

36

keys. If you cannot remember these key combinations don't worry, there is always another way of carrying out their functions. All of the above can be selected from the dialogue box activated with the **Insert**, **Special Character** command. When you have finished, save the document using the **File, Save As** command, calling it LETTER1.

To improve the layout of the letter we will use some of the commands in the **Format** sub-menu and also some of the Toolbar and Quick key options.

First select the top five lines containing the address and date (the easiest way of doing this is to click the mouse alongside line one, in the left margin, and drag it down to line 5) and then select the **Format**, **Paragraph**, **Indents and Alignment**, command to open the box below. Select the **Alignment** as **Right** as shown and press **OK**.

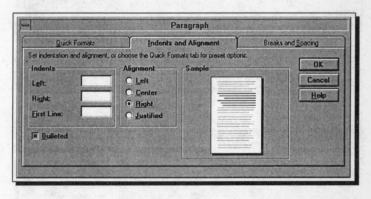

The whole block should now be 'right justified'. By default paragraphs are 'left justified'. While the block is still highlighted click the mouse on the Left Align icon of the Toolbar. Now press the <Ctrl+R> keys and you should be back with a right justified address.

Then select the Ref.... line of text and press **Format**, **Paragraph**, **Indents and Alignment**, **Center** (or the quick keys <Ctrl+E>, or the Centre Align Toolbar icon) to centre the line between the left and right margins. While the selection highlight is still active press **Format**, **Font and Style**, **Underline** (or <Ctrl+U>, or the Underline icon on the Toolbar) to underline the reference. By now you have probably accepted that the Toolbar is by far the most convenient way of carrying out these enhancement functions. If you repeat the Toolbar click, while the highlight is still active, the feature is turned off again; they act as toggle functions.

Next, select the words 'recent letter' and press <Ctrl+B>, or the Bold icon, to embolden them. Finally, select the section 'Micro Users Journal' and change them to italics by pressing **Format**, **Font and Style**, **Italic,** or <Ctrl+I>, or the Italic icon.

The letter now looks very different and should be similar to LETTER2.WPS shown below.

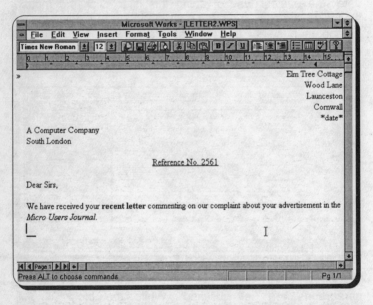

What a difference with only a few keystrokes! Note that when the cursor is in text that has been enhanced, the relevant icon on the Toolbar appears 'depressed'. In the above example the Left Align icon is selected. These status indicators are useful when the enhancements are not obvious from the screen text.

Fonts:

A font is a typeface with a specific design. In Works for Windows you can print text in any fonts, or colours, which are supported by your printer, the fonts are also shown on the

WYSIWYG (what you see is what you get) editing screens (except for Draft View).

To change the font, size, colour or enhancements of specific text in a document, first select the text. Choose the **Format, Font & Style** command, and make selections in the opened dialogue box, as shown below.

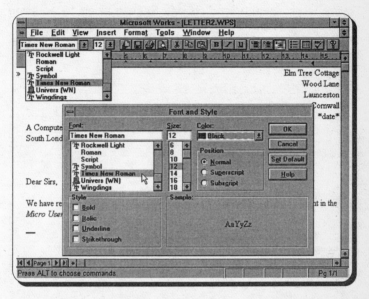

You can also, of course, change the font and size of selected text from the Font Name and Font Size icons. Clicking the arrow alongside each opens up a menu of available options.

The composite screen, made up above, shows both methods of changing the font and font size of selected text. You will not be able to get them both on the screen at the same time, though, so do not bother trying.

The Toolbar icons are by far the best option, as is obvious by the way Microsoft have buried the text formatting commands so deeply in the menu system.

Works measures font sizes in points, where one point is 1/72nd of an inch. You will need to study your printer manual and experiment with these commands to make the most of this Works facility.

One thing to remember is that a printed page usually looks better if you use different fonts and sizes sparingly.

3. ADVANCED WP FEATURES

Paragraph Formatting

Works for Windows defines a paragraph, as any text which is followed by a paragraph mark (which appears as a '¶' character on the screen, but only when switched on). So single line titles, as well as long typed text, can form paragraphs. Paragraph markers are not normally shown in Works, but toggling the **View**, **All Characters** command, will toggle them on and off. The example below shows our file MEMO1.WPS with formatting characters switched on. This facility can be very useful when you are laying out a complicated page of data. Note how blank space characters show as a '·' character.

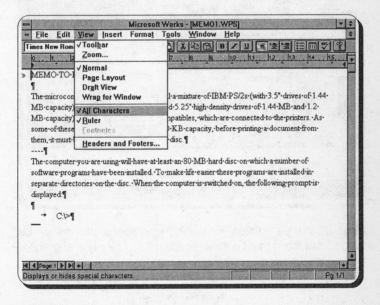

A paragraph marker is placed in a document every time <Enter> is pressed. All paragraph formatting, such as alignment, justification, centring, indenting and line spacing, is stored in the marker for the particular paragraph. If this marker is deleted, or moved, the formatting will be deleted or moved with it.

Indenting Text:

Most documents with lists, or numbered sections, will require some form of paragraph indenting. An indent is the space between the margin and the edge of the text in the paragraph. This can be on the left or right side of the page.

Retrieve the file MEMO1.WPS and type '1. ' and '2. ' before the first words of the two main text paragraphs. Select the two paragraphs and press **Format**, **Paragraph**, **Indents and Alignment** to open the dialogue box below.

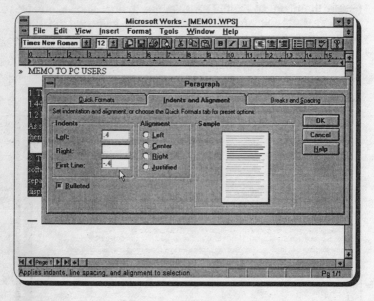

Most of the paragraph formatting operations can either be carried out from the Toolbar, or from this box. The alignment box offers:

Left	Smooth left edge, ragged right
Center	Text centred on line
Right	Smooth right edge, ragged left
Justified	Smooth left and right edges

To create left or right indents for the whole paragraph, type the amount of indent in the respective space, in centimetres. If only the first line is to be indented, type the amount needed in the **First Line**, **Indents** space.

If you select the box tab **Breaks and Spacing** you will find options to fully control the spacing between lines and paragraphs. To keep a paragraph intact on one page, check the **Don't break paragraph** box. Select **Keep paragraph with next** to keep two paragraphs together on a page.

Hanging Indents:

The dialogue box on the previous page is set up to produce hanging indents, so that the paragraph numbers show up clearly at the left of the paragraphs.

To do this you should type the same value in the **First Line**, **Indents** space - with a negative sign in front - as that typed in the **Left**, **Indents** space. When you have finished, and saved the document as MEMO2.WPS, your screen should look the same as that shown below.

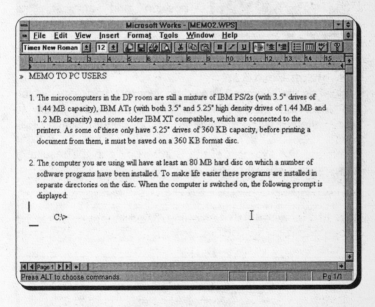

Hanging indents can also be created with the quick key combination <Ctrl+H>. If no dialogue box has previously been completed, the indents are set to the next tab stop. <Ctrl+G> will remove the hanging indent. Two fascinating key combinations to play with are those to produce and remove nested indents - <Ctrl+N> and <Ctrl+M>. These move the whole paragraph holding the cursor, to the next tab stop, to the right or left respectively, and maintain any hanging indents. With the careful use of these keys and the Bullets icon, lists and outlines are easy and fun to prepare.

Indenting with the Ruler:

If you look carefully at the Ruler at the top of the screen, after

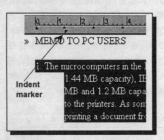

you have placed an indent, you should see that an indent marker has been placed on it. This gives you another way of quickly setting and adjusting indents. You simply drag the marker to the new indent position and any selected paragraphs will be indented, as shown here.

Paragraph Borders:

As well as the Microsoft Draw and WordArt packages, which are described later, Works for Windows has the facility to place different types of lines at the top, bottom, sides, or all round selected paragraphs, with the **Format, Border** command. An example of the Border box and the results of its settings is shown below.

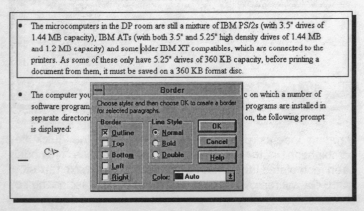

44

First, select the paragraphs you want to enhance, then in the Border box turn on the border you want, in the Line style box select either **Normal**, **Bold** or **Double** and then press <Enter>, or select **OK**. To remove borders you must cancel the selections made in these boxes.

Printing Documents

When Microsoft Windows was first installed on your computer the printers you intend to use should have been selected, and the SETUP program should have installed the appropriate printer drivers. Before printing for the first time from Works for Windows, you would be wise to ensure that your printer is in fact properly installed.

To do this open the Window's Control Panel, as described at the end of Chapter 1 and double-click on the 'Printers' icon. This will open the **Printers** box shown below.

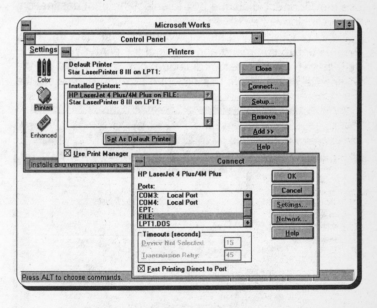

Here, two printer drivers have been installed; a Star LaserPrinter as the 'default', configured for output via the computer parallel printer port LPT1, and an HP LaserJet, configured to print to a disc file. Your selections will, obviously, not be the same.

Best printed output results are usually obtained when using a laser printer. So, if you want to produce high-quality documents, and you have access to a laser printer (even if it is not connected to your computer and does not itself have access to Works), then install the laser printer as an additional printer to be used with Windows and configure it to print to 'File', as shown here.

To install an extra printer press the **Add** button in the 'Printers' dialogue box, choose a printer from the list displayed, and select **Install**. Each time you choose to install a different printer, Windows will ask you to insert a particular disc in the A: drive, so that the appropriate printer driver (a file containing the instructions Windows needs to control that printer) can be copied to your computer's hard disc. Then use the 'Connect' dialogue box to select the print destination, as shown above.

Next, reactivate Works for Windows and use the **File, Printer Setup** command and highlight the printer you want to use in the Printer Setup dialogue box, as shown in the composite below. From this dialogue box you can select the

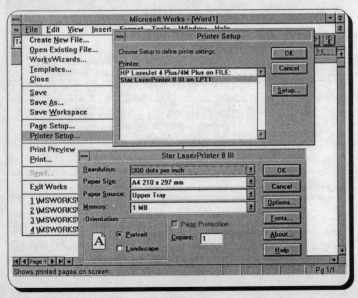

default printer or any other installed printer. Next, press **Setup,** select the paper size and orientation needed, and then either press **OK** to confirm your selection, or **Cancel** to abort the procedure.

Now your printer is set up you can, at any time, use the **File, Print** command from the Works for Windows menu bar, or <Ctrl+P>, which both open the 'Print' box, shown below.

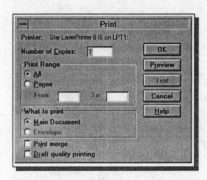

The settings in this box allow you to select the number of copies, and which pages, are printed. **Draft quality printing** gives you a rapid hard copy, without fonts, enhancements or graphics. Finally select **OK**, to send print output from Works for Windows to your selected destination, either the printer connected to your computer, or to an encoded file on disc.

The Print icon on the Toolbar sends the current document to the printer using the active settings. It does not give you access to the Print box.

Printing from a File:

An encoded print file, as described above, has all the printer commands embedded in it and can be printed on, for example, a laser printer by using the simple DOS command

```
COPY Filename LPT1 /B
```

to copy the file to the printer, from the computer connected to it. Works for Windows, or indeed Windows, do not need to be running, or even installed, on this computer at all.

Do remember that, whenever you change printers, the appearance of your document may change, as Works uses the fonts available with the newly selected printer. This can affect the line lengths, which in turn will affect both tabulation and pagination of your document.

Page Setup:

The next operation, to make sure your printer is happy with your document settings, is to set up Works for the paper and margin layout you want to use. The **File**, **Page Setup** command opens the tabbed dialogue box shown here. The settings in the three sections of this box are the UK default.

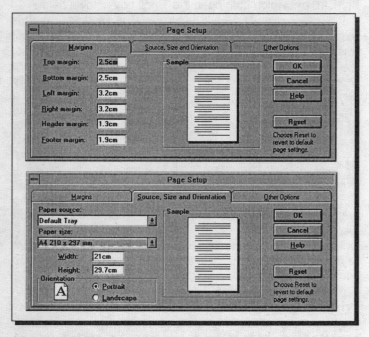

The **Margins** section includes settings for **Top, Bottom, Left** and **Right** margins, which are the non-print areas required on each edge of the paper. The **Header margin** is that required between the top of the page and the header line. The **Footer margin** is that between the bottom of the page and the footer line.

The **Source, Size and Orientation** section defaults to A4 size paper (11.69" x 8.27"). If you want to use a different size paper just select a standard size from the **Paper size** drop down list, or type in new dimensions for **Width** and **Height**. The default orientation is **Portrait** mode with the height of a page being greater than the width.

The **Other Options** section gives you control over the **1st page number** which will normally be '1' unless you break up a piece of work into parts, or chapters, and have each one in a separate document file. This facility then allows you to adjust the page numbering of each.

Print Preview:

Works gives you an easy way of checking what your printer will produce with the **File**, **Print Preview** command. It lets you see a screen view of what the printed page should look like, similar to that shown below.

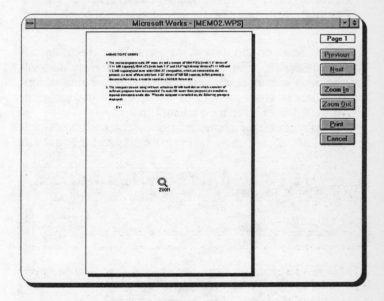

You can **Zoom In** or **Zoom Out**, or click the ZOOM mouse pointer over a section of the page, to see your work at different magnification levels, and step through a multi-page document with the **Previous** or **Next** buttons. If you are happy with the preview press **Print** to print the selected pages, otherwise press **Cancel** to exit Preview.

Text Enhancement

Tab Settings:

Works for Windows defaults to left aligned tabs every 1.3cm, or 0.5in, across the page. For most purposes these will be adequate, but if you need to generate lists, or tables, indexes, etc., the custom tab facility should prove useful. There are four types of custom tab stops:

Left	Text aligns to the right of tab
Right	Text aligns to the left of tab
Center	Text centres on tab stop
Decimal	Text aligns at a decimal point

Tabs are shown on the ruler at the top of the screen, as can be seen below. All default tabs to the left of a new custom tab are removed automatically. You can also select one of four types of leader characters to fill the space to the tab spot. This is useful when preparing contents pages.

The example below shows part of a contents page which has two **Left** aligned tabs for the subjects, and a **Right** tab

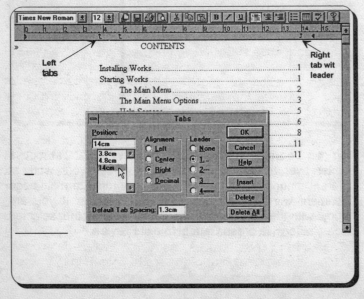

50

with a dot leader for the page numbers. To set custom tab stops, select the required paragraph, or the whole document, and either double click your mouse on the ruler, or choose **Format, Tabs**. A dialogue box like the one shown on the previous page will open.

If necessary, type the tab **Position** in the text box, select the options needed from the **Alignment** and **Leader** boxes and choose **Insert** to place the tab on the ruler. This operation can be repeated for as many tabs as are required. Use the **Delete**, or **Delete All** buttons to remove one tab, or all the tabs, from the ruler.

Tables of figures can be created, and adjusted, by the careful use of tab settings. Use decimal, or right aligned tab stops, for columns of figures. It is an easy matter to readjust the width of columns by resetting the tabs, even after the table has been created.

Headers and Footers:

In a printed document a header is text that appears at the top of each page of the document, whilst a footer appears at the bottom. These can be used to add page numbers, titles, dates and times to your documents. In the word processor it is possible to add two kinds of headers and footers - both paragraph and standard types.

Standard ones are typed in a dialogue box, and alignment characters are required to force their printed positions. Paragraph headers and footers have a special paragraph for each, placed at the top of the document, and text, or a graphic, can be added and formatted as in the rest of the document.

Header and footer paragraphs are shown in the next example. These were added to the file MEMO2.WPS, in Normal View mode, by choosing the **View**, **Headers & Footers** command, turning on the **Use header & footer paragraphs** check box, and pressing <Enter>.

Note that the program turns on the separate header and footer paragraphs (and places an 'H' and an 'F' at the left margin), and also places an automatic page number placeholder in the centre of the footer line. (Page - *page*). This will print the correct page number on every page. If page numbering is not required this can be deleted, or the code can be moved to another location on the header or footer lines.

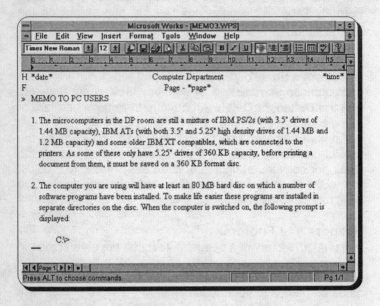

Move the cursor to the start of the header paragraph and add the date special command <Ctrl+D>. This adds *date* to the screen, but will print the current date on paper. Press <Tab> and the cursor is automatically centred on the line. Add a title and press <Tab> again to bring the cursor to the right hand side of the page. Add the time special command <Ctrl+T>, and save as MEMO3.

Your screen should now look like that shown above. Use the **File**, **Print Preview** command to quickly check the printed result. If you want, you can add enhancements, or change the fonts of the header and footer text.

In the Works for Windows Spreadsheet and Database tools only standard headers and footers can be used. As these can also be used in the Word Processor, we will describe them here. Choose **View**, **Headers & Footers,** as before, and type the required text in the two boxes. You can align parts of a standard header or footer, and include other items automatically, by typing any of the special codes from the following list in with the text. Note that, unless you change the alignment, standard headers and footers are automatically centred.

Operation	*Special Code*
To align following text	&l or &r
at left or right margin	
To centre the following text	&c
To print page number	&p
To print filename	&f
To print date	&d
To print long date format	&n
To print time	&t
To print an ampersand	&&

As many of these codes as required, can be placed on a single header or footer line. The following example shows the **Header** codes entered and the resulting header with the screen in Page Layout Mode and a Zoom factor of 80.

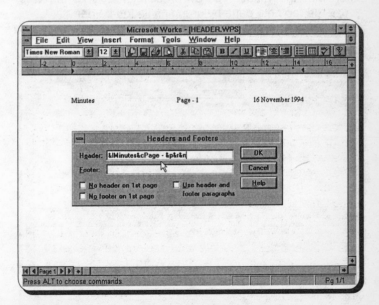

Footnotes:

A useful feature in Works for Windows is the ability to place reference marks, or numbers, anywhere in a document. Text can be 'attached' to each reference, which will automatically be printed at the end of the relevant page. This operation is carried out with the **Insert**, **Footnote** command.

Footnotes are automatically numbered, and renumbered if edited, but you can also specify other reference marks (such as * or $, for example).

To create a footnote, move the cursor to the position in the document where the reference mark is needed, choose **Insert**, **Footnote,** alter the dialogue box if you want to force a mark instead of a numbered reference, and select **OK**, or you could use the WorksWizard offered in the box.

If **Numbered** is selected in the box, the next consecutive footnote number is placed at the cursor and the footnote pane is opened in the bottom half of the screen. Type the reference text in this pane, and format, or enhance it, if required. You can move the cursor back to the document either with the mouse, or by pressing **F6**. You can also re-size the footnote pane by dragging its top border.

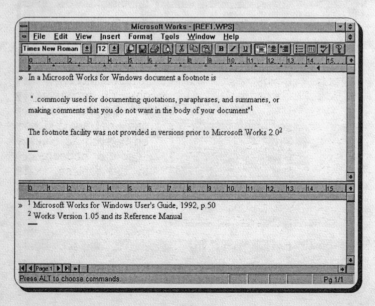

Once placed, footnote reference marks are always shown in the document. The footnote text itself can be shown, or switched off, by toggling the **View**, **Show Footnotes** command. In the previous example this option has been selected in Normal View mode.

Footnote text can be edited, the same as any other text, once the footnote pane is opened. Reference marks can also be moved, copied or deleted, and Works for Windows will look after the positioning of the attached text.

Endnotes:

When you print a document that contains footnotes, they are placed at the bottom of the page holding the reference point. To force your reference text to be printed at the end of the main body of the document text, place them as described above, but check the **File**, **Page Setup**, **Print footnotes at end of document** option.

Your final printed presentation of these endnotes will be improved if you place blank lines at the end of the document text. Without these the footnote text will be printed immediately under the last line of document text. Any reference heading required should be placed after these blank lines.

Searching for and Replacing Text:

Works allows you to search for specifically selected text, or character combinations. In the search mode, actioned with the **Edit**, **Find** command, it will highlight each occurrence in

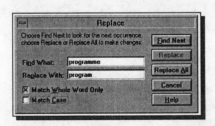

turn so that you can carry out some action on it, such as change its font or appearance. In the replace mode you specify what replacement is to be automatically carried out. For example, in a long book chapter you may decide to replace every occurrence of the word 'programme' with the word 'program'. This is very easy to do. First go to the beginning of the file, as search only operates in a forward direction, then choose

Edit, **Replace**. In the **Find What** box, type **programme**, and in the **Replace With** box type **program**. To make sure that part words are not selected, choose the **Match Whole Word Only** option, and then click the **Find Next** button. The first match will be highlighted in the document then either choose **Replace**, to change once, or **<Replace All>** for automatic replacement.

Works automatically matches the capitalisation of any text it replaces. If the replaced word is at the beginning of a sentence it will capitalise the first letter. If you select the **Match Case** option, only text with the exactly specified case letters will be selected.

You can search for, and replace, special characters, or a combination of text and special characters (for example, tab or paragraph marks, or white space). White space is a combination of any number of consecutive spaces and tab marks. A very useful example of this is when you have imported columnar data from another file, and the columns are separated with spaces; you can search for white space, and replace it with a tab, to realign the columns.

Another example would be searching for a word, which occurs at the beginning of a paragraph, or after a tab.

The list below gives the key combinations of special characters to type into search and replace boxes.

To type the caret (^) character, press **Shift+6.**

To search for or replace	Type
Tab mark	^t
Paragraph mark	^p
End-of-line mark	^n
Manual page break mark	^d
Non-breaking space	^s
Caret (^)	^^
Question mark (?)	^?
White space	^w
Any character (wild card)	?
Extended ANSI character	^NUM

The *NUM* above represents the code entered from the computer numeric keypad with the <Alt> key depressed.

Using the Spell Checker:

If you have a problem with spelling, the spell checker in Works for Windows will be a popular part of the package! It will search for wrongly spelled words, words with incorrect capitalisation, incorrect hyphenation, and repeated words, such as 'if if'. It has a built-in dictionary of 113,664 words, according to the Help documentation, and you can add other words that you may need to check for in the future.

To check the spelling of a whole document, move the cursor to the beginning with <Ctrl+Home>. Alternatively, you can select the text you want checked. In either case, invoke the checker by choosing **Tools**, **Spelling**, or by clicking the Spelling Checker icon. When a word that is not recognised is found, a box appears as shown in the example below.

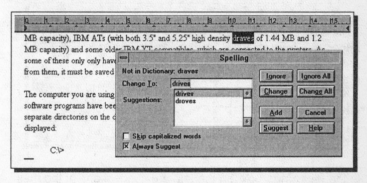

A problem message will appear in the top left corner of the box, the suspect word will be highlighted in the document, and will also be placed in the **Change To** box.

You have several options now:

a. To leave the word unchanged choose **Ignore**

b. To change the word, edit, or retype it, in the box, and choose **Change,** or **Change All** to change all instances of that word.

c. Choose **Suggest,** to view a list of proposed spellings from the dictionary, select one and then choose **Change.**

d. To add an edited word to the dictionary, choose **Add.**

When you have made your choice, the program continues searching the rest of the document. To leave the checker at any time simply choose **Cancel**. We must admit we had trouble getting the Spell Checker to pick up all cases of word duplication.

Using the Thesaurus:

To help you with composing your documents Works has a built-in 190,000 word thesaurus. With this you should be able to find a synonym, or word with a similar meaning, for most words. First select the word you want to change, and choose **Tools**, **Thesaurus.** The dialogue box with two main sections comes onto the screen, as shown below.

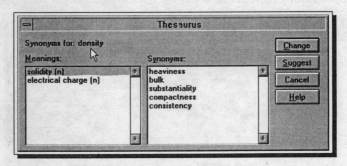

In the **Meanings** box, on the left, are suggestions of the main meanings of the selected word. Depending on the context in the document, you need to select one of these meanings, and then look in the **Synonyms** box for a list of possible replacement words.

In the example shown 'density' was the word highlighted in the document. The noun 'solidity' was selected from the **Meanings** list which produced the five synonyms shown. Sometimes the logic of the choices has to make you smile.

If you select one of the synonyms and press **Suggest** you should get more alternatives to look at.

To replace the original word highlighted in your document, select the best alternative and choose **Change.**

Word Count:

Works for Windows includes the facility to count the words in a document, or block of selected text. This can be useful if you are working on an assignment that requires a specific number of words. The program considers a word to be any text between two space characters.

Select the text to be counted and use the **Tools**, **Word Count** command. If no text is selected the whole document will be counted, including footnotes, headers and footers.

Adding a Note to your Document

A very useful, if rather 'flamboyant', facility added to Works for Windows is the ability to add 'pop-up' notes anywhere in your documents. Place the cursor where you want a Note to be placed and action the **Insert**, **Note-It** command. The following dialogue box is opened.

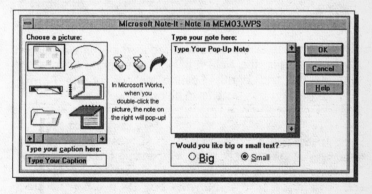

The **Choose a picture** box gives you the amazing choice of 58 different note types. If it turns you on, you can liven up your document no end! To place a caption under the displayed note, type the required text in the **Type your caption here** text box. The main text to be 'hidden' in the note is typed in the **Type your note here** box. Select the size of Note text you want from the **Big** and **Small** options and finally press **OK** to place your note.

At any time in the future the note text can be read by double clicking on the note, as shown in the example on the next page.

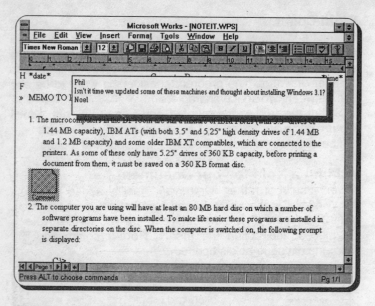

The size of the Note above was reduced after it was placed, by first selecting the Note graphic and entering 50% in both the **Height** and **Width Scaling** options of the **Format, Picture/Object** box, as shown below.

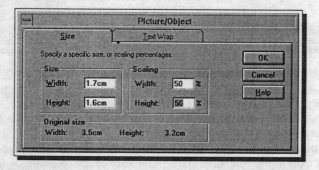

Notes can be very useful if several people are editing a document and they want to make comments, for the others to see.

Adding WordArt to your Document

Another addition to Version 3.0 of the Works for Windows package is the WordArt facility which lets you easily create quite eye-catching title lines for your documents. To use it, place the insertion point where you want the heading and use the **Insert**, **WordArt** command. Type your heading text and note that a new Toolbar has been added to the screen, as shown below.

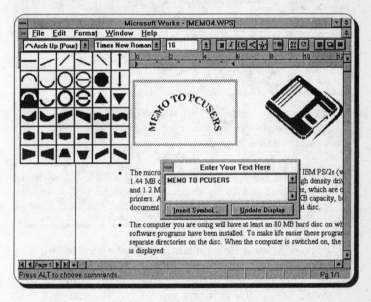

This shows the shapes available in the drop down menu opened on the left of the bar. A quick way of seeing the other Toolbar functions is to press **F1** while in WordArt mode and select the green hypertext link '*A Description of WordArt Special Text Effects* '.

When your heading looks the way you want, simply click the pointer outside the dialogue box to return to your document, which should now have the new heading placed on it. You can edit a WordArt graphic at any time by double-clicking it.

To change the position of any Works graphic, select it and use the **Format**, **Picture/Object**, **Text Wrap**, **Absolute** command and then drag it across the page.

61

Adding a Drawing to a Document

You may have noticed that the previous example screen showed a floppy disc graphic in the document. This was easily added with the **Insert**, **ClipArt** command, which opens the Microsoft ClipArt Gallery shown below.

This even includes a **Helpful Hint** to tell you what to do!

ClipArt consists of picture images, usually professionally created. You can add more to the Gallery, and change categories, etc., in the **Options** box.

It is also possible to Paste a graphic from the Windows clipboard into your document. It will be placed, as with ClipArt, into its own frame.

Once your graphic is placed in the document and selected (by clicking it), you can move, copy, Drag and Drop and delete it the same as you can with selected text. You may need to set **Text Wrap**, **Absolute** as described on the last page, or the graphic will only flow with its surrounding text.

4. MICROSOFT DRAW

The Drawing Tool

Works for Windows also includes Microsoft Draw, a quite comprehensive drawing and graphics manipulation package. This is actually a separate program which can be accessed from the Works for Windows word processing tool. You can import existing 'clip art' into a document with the Microsoft Draw tool, which can also be used to create, or edit, drawings consisting of lines, arcs, ellipses, text and rectangles. The Draw tool is opened by either using the **Drawing** option from the **Insert** menu of the Word Processor, or double-clicking within an existing picture in a document. When opened from the menu, the drawing tool runs in a separate window, as shown below. When it is closed any graphics created will be embedded in the document at the cursor position.

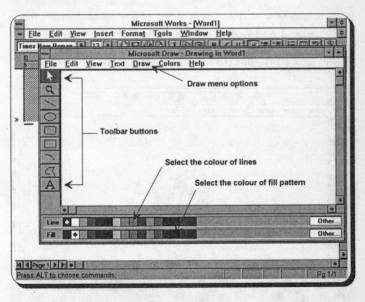

Microsoft Draw is an OLE (object linking and embedding) type of Windows program, which is also included with Word for Windows.

Importing a Picture:

The quickest way to get some results from Draw is to load an existing graphic from disc. When Works for Windows was installed on your computer some picture files should have been placed in the **clipart** subdirectory of \MSWORKS. Open a new document in the Word processor and activate Draw with the **Insert**, **Drawing** command, as described. You will see that Draw has its own menu system, which we will describe in more detail later on. At this stage, open the **File** sub-menu and select **Import Picture**, the dialogue box shown here is opened. Click on 'clipart' in the **Directories** list box and you should open a list of available graphic files. Select one of these, in our case 'soccer.wmf', and press **OK** to import the drawing into the Draw window. Your screen should look something like that shown below.

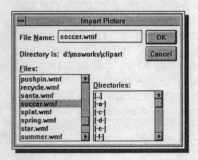

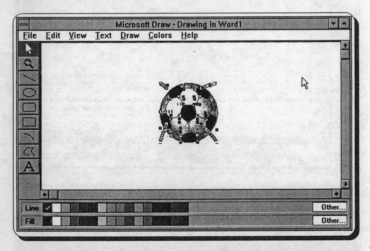

To return to your document use the **File**, **Exit and Return to Word 1** command from the Draw menu system. If you had actually named your original document, this name would show in the above command, in place of **Word 1**. Select **Yes** to update your document and the image will be placed at the cursor position.

The cursor will show as a long vertical line blinking to the left of the inserted image. Press <Ctrl+E> to centre the graphic, <End> to move the cursor past it and then <Enter> to move to a new line below it. You can now continue as usual. The result of the above commands is shown below, maybe an ideal logo for a Premier League club?

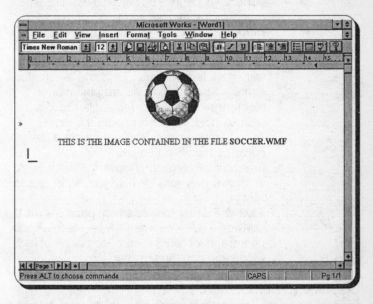

Using the Microsoft Draw tool, you can also create and select objects in a picture, then copy and move them, or change their size, shape and colour, etc. These options can be carried out either by using the toolbar on the left of the Draw screen, or by using the Draw pull-down menus.

Using the Draw Toolbar:
Works provides a variety of buttons in the Toolbar on the left of the Draw screen, both for creating objects such as lines, circles, squares, or text objects and for manipulating these

objects, once they have been selected. The buttons on the Draw toolbar are:

Selection Arrow - Selects or sizes an object, or group of objects.

Magnifying Glass - Selects a specified area of a picture and magnifies it.

Line - Draws a straight line in the direction you drag the mouse. To draw a line at a perfect 45 degree angle, hold <Shift> while dragging the mouse.

Ellipse - Draws an ellipse. To draw a circle, hold <Shift> while dragging the mouse.

Rounded Rectangle - Draws a rectangle with rounded corners. To draw a rounded square, hold <Shift> and drag the mouse.

Rectangle - Draws a rectangle. To draw a square, hold <Shift> and drag the mouse.

Arc - Draws an arc. You can create a Bezier curve by modifying an arc.

Freehand/Polygon - Draws freehand lines, or draws polygons. When you finish, press <Esc>.

Text - Places the insertion point inside a drawing so you can type text, each paragraph of which will become an object, which you can then manipulate.

Draw Menu Commands:

Most of the menu commands available with Microsoft Draw are self-explanatory. The few that are not, are listed below with details of their function.

Command	Function
File, Update	Updates the drawing in the Works for Windows document.
File, Import Picture	Loads a graphic file from disc to the Draw package.
File, Exit & Return	Closes Draw and returns control to Works for Windows.

66

Draw, Group	Groups the selected objects.
Draw, Ungroup	Ungroups the selected objects.
Draw, Framed	Draws an outline frame around the selected object.
Draw, Filled	Changes the fill pattern of the selected object to the current fill pattern.
Draw, Pattern	Displays colour and fill pattern options.
Draw, Line Style	Displays line styles available and thickness of lines.
Draw, Snap to Grid	Aligns objects automatically, or manually, on the grid.
Draw, Show Guides	Displays vertical and horizontal guide lines.
Draw, Rotate/Flip	Rotates/flips the selected object, or group of objects, clockwise or anticlockwise.

Creating a Drawing:

To create an object, click on the required Draw button, such as the ellipse, position the mouse pointer where you want to create the object on the screen, and then drag the mouse to draw the object. Hold the <Shift> key while you drag the mouse to create a perfect circle, square, or rounded square. If you do not hold <Shift>, Draw creates an ellipse, a rectangle, or a rounded rectangle.

You can use the freehand/polygon Draw button to create freehand objects. First click on the freehand button, then position the mouse pointer where you want to create the object on the screen. If you then press the left mouse button and keep it pressed, the mouse pointer changes to the shape of a pencil with which you can draw freehand. If, on the other hand, you click the left mouse button, the edge of the line attaches itself on the drawing area, at the point of contact, and the pointer changes to a crosshair. A straight line can then be drawn between that point and the next point on which you happen to click the mouse button. In this way you can draw polygons. When you finish drawing with either of these two methods, press the <Esc> key.

Editing a Drawing:

To select an object, first click the 'Selection Arrow' button and then click the desired object. Draw displays black handles around the object selected.

You can move an object, or multiple objects, within a drawing by selecting them and dragging them to the desired position. To copy an object, click at the object, then use the **Edit, Copy / Edit, Paste** commands.

To size an object within Draw, position the mouse pointer on a black handle and then drag the handle until the object is the desired shape and size.

To delete an object, select the object and press <Del>. To delete a drawing, hold the <Shift> key down and click each object in turn that makes up the drawing, then press <Del>. You could also use instead the **Edit, Select All** command, and then press <Del>.

Using Layered Drawings:

You can use Draw's **Edit**, **Bring to Front** or **Send to Back** commands to determine the order of layered drawings. Drawings or pictures layered on top of each other can create useful visual effects, provided you remember that the top drawing/picture obscures the one below it.

Using Line and Fill:

You can use the 'Line' and 'Fill' colour palette at the bottom of Draw's screen, to specify the colour of the lines and the colour of the fill pattern for selected drawings/pictures. The first time you access Microsoft Draw, the line colour is black and the fill pattern is transparent.

We will leave it up to you to find practical uses for all the above features of the Draw package. Have fun.

5. THE WORKS SPREADSHEET

When you first enter the Works for Windows spreadsheet, the program sets up a huge electronic page, or worksheet, in your computer's memory, many times larger than the small part shown on the screen. Individual cells are identified by column and row location (in that order), with the present size extending to 256 columns by a massive 16,384 rows. The columns are labelled from A to Z, followed by AA to AZ, BA to BZ, and so on, to IV, while the rows are numbered from 1 to 16,384.

Using the **File, Create New File** command and selecting the **Spreadsheet** option from the dialogue box, displays the following screen:

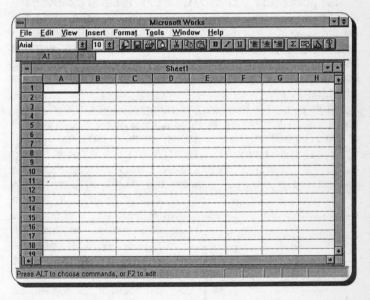

A worksheet can be thought of as a two-dimensional table made up of rows and columns. The point where a row and column intersect is called a cell, while the reference points of a cell are known as the cell address. The active cell (A1 when you first enter the program) is highlighted.

Worksheet Navigation

Navigation around the worksheet is achieved by the use of the four arrow keys. Each time one of these keys is pressed, the active cell moves one position right, down, left or up, depending on which arrow key was pressed. The <PgDn> and <PgUp> keys can also be used to move vertically one full page at a time, while the <Ctrl+PgDn> and <Ctrl+PgUp> key combinations can be used to move horizontally one full page at a time. Pressing the arrow keys while holding down the <Ctrl> key causes the active cell to be moved to the extremities of the worksheet. For example, <Ctrl+→> moves the active cell to the IV column, while <Ctrl+↓> moves the active cell to the 16,384th row.

You can move the active cell with a mouse by moving the mouse pointer to the cell you want to activate and clicking the left mouse button. If the cell is not visible, then move the window by clicking on the scroll bar arrowhead that points in the direction you want to move, until the cell you want to activate is visible. To move a page at a time, click in the scroll bar itself, or for larger moves, drag the scroll box in the scroll bar.

When you have finished navigating around the worksheet, press the <Ctrl+Home> keys which will move the active cell to the A1 position. This is known as the 'Home' position. If you press the <Home> key by itself, the active cell is moved to the 1st column of the particular row. Note that there are several areas on your screen; the displayed area within which you can move the active cell is referred to as the working area of the worksheet, while the letters and numbers in the border around the displayed portion of the worksheet form the reference points.

The location of the active cell is constantly monitored in the Cell Reference Area at the left end of the Formula Bar, below the Toolbar. If you type text in the active cell, what you type appears in both the formula bar and in the cell itself. Typing a formula which is preceded by the equals sign (=) to, say, add the contents of two cells, causes the actual formula to appear in the 'formula bar', while the result of the actual calculation appears in the active cell when the <Enter> key or button is pressed.

The GOTO Command:

Sometimes it is necessary to move to a specific address in the worksheet which, however, is so far from your present position that using the arrow keys might take far too long to get there. To this end, Works has implemented the **F5** function key as a 'go to' command. For example, to jump to position HZ4000, press the **F5** key, which will cause Works to ask for the address of the cell to which it is to jump. This request appears in a dialogue box.

Now, typing HZ4000 and pressing <Enter>, causes the active cell to jump to that cell address. To specify a cell address, you must always key one or two letters followed by a number. The letters can range from A to IV corresponding to a column, while the numbers can range from 1 to 16,384 corresponding to a row. Specifying a column or row outside this range will cause an error message to be displayed in the dialogue box. To clear the error, press <Enter>, or the <Esc> key; the <Esc> key can also be used to cancel a command and escape from a situation before an error occurs.

Entering Information

We will now investigate how information can be entered into the worksheet. But first, return to the Home (A1) position by pressing <Ctrl+Home>, then type in the words:

```
PROJECT ANALYSIS
```

As you type, the characters appear in both the 'formula bar' and the active cell window.

If you make a mistake, press the <BkSp> key to erase the previous letter or the <Esc> key to start again. When you have finished, press <Enter>. Note that what you have just typed in has been entered in cell A1, even though part of the word ANALYSIS appears to be in cell B1. If you use the right arrow key to move the active cell to B1 you will see that the cell is indeed empty.

Note that the text displayed in the 'formula bar' is prefixed by double quotation marks (") which were added automatically by the program to indicate that the entry is a 'label' and not a number, or a date. Thus, typing a letter at the beginning of an entry into a cell results in a 'label' being formed. If the length of a label is longer than the width of a cell, it will continue into the next cell to the right of the current active cell, provided that cell is empty, otherwise the displayed label will be truncated.

To edit information already in a cell, move the pointer to the appropriate cell and either press the **F2** function key, or click in the 'formula bar'. The cursor keys, the <Home> and <End> keys, as well as the <Ins> and <Del> keys can be used to move the cursor and/or edit the information displayed in the 'formula bar', as required. After such editing of information in the formula bar, you must either press the <Enter> key, or click the '√' button on the formula bar, to enter it in the active cell.

Now use the arrow keys to move the active cell to B3 and type

    "Jan

Then press the right-arrow key, which will automatically enter the abbreviation 'Jan' into the cell, as a label, and will also move the active cell to position C3. Had we only typed Jan (without the double quotes prefix) on pressing either <Enter> or the right-arrow key, the word 'January' would have appeared automatically in the cell, as a date. In cell C3, type

    "Feb

and again press the right-arrow key.

The looks of a worksheet can be enhanced considerably by placing lines, or cell borders, to separate information in different rows. Select the cells A4 to C4 (from the keyboard use the <Shift+Right> keystroke; with the mouse drag the active cell) and choose the **Format**, **Border** menu command. This opens the Border dialogue box, from which you can place any combination of lines along the borders of selected cells. In our case, select **Top** and the heavy **Line Style** option and press **OK** to accept the settings.

Finally, type in the label and amounts earned in columns A, B and C of row 5, as shown in the full screen dump below.

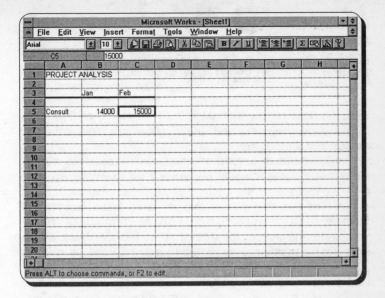

Note how the labels 'Jan' and 'Feb' do not appear above the numbers 14000 and 15000. This is because by default, labels are left justified, while numbers are right justified.

Changing Text Alignment and Fonts:
One way of improving the looks of this worksheet is to also right justify the labels 'Jan' and 'Feb' within their respective cells. To do this, move the active cell to B3 and mark the range B3 to C3 (from the keyboard use the <Shift+→> keystroke; with the mouse drag the active cell), choose the **Format, Alignment** command, then select the **Right** option listed in the 'Alignment' dialogue box and press <Enter>. The

 labels should now appear right justified within their cells. An easier way to carry out this operation is to select the cells and click the Right Align Toolbar icon, shown here.

We could further improve the looks of the worksheet by choosing a different font for the heading 'Project Analysis'. To achieve this, move the active cell to A1, choose the **Format, Font and Style** command, then select Courier, **Size** 8 and **Italic**, from the options listed in the displayed dialogue box,

73

and press <Enter>. The heading will now appear in Courier 8, Italic font.

Once again the Toolbar gives a much quicker way of carrying out these operations. Simply click the down arrow alongside the Font Name or Font Size icons, shown above, and make your selection from the menus that drop down.

Finally, since the entered numbers in cells B5 to C5 represent money, it would be better if these were displayed with two digits after the decimal point and prefixed with the £ sign. To do this, move the active cell to B5 and select the cell block B5 to C5, then choose the **Format, Number, Currency** command and accept the default number of decimals, which is 2. This formatting operation can also be done by clicking the Currency Toolbar icon, shown here, which formats selected cells to currency with 2 decimal places. The numbers within the marked worksheet range should now be displayed in the new format. If the width of the relevant cells had not been large enough to accommodate all the digits of the new format, they would have been filled with the hash character (#) to indicate insufficient space. The columns would then need to be widened.

Changing the Column Width:

To change the width of a given column or a number of columns, activate a cell in the relevant column, or block the number of required column cells, use the **Format** command and select the **Column Width** option from the pull-down sub-menu. This causes a dialogue box to be displayed with the default column width offered as 10 characters. Typing 12 and pressing <Enter>, changes the width of the selected columns to 12 characters.

A quicker method of doing this, if you prefer, is to position the mouse pointer in the column headings at the top of the working area. It will change shape as you move it over the border of two columns. Dragging this new pointer right or left, will widen, or narrow, the column to the left.

If the currency symbol displays as a '$' don't panic, it just means your version of Windows is not set up for the UK. To remedy this from within Works for Windows, hold down the <Alt> key and repeatedly press the <Tab> key until the Program Manager option is offered. Releasing both keys will then open the Program Manager window.

Open the Control Panel and double click on the International icon. Make sure that 'United Kingdom' is selected in the **Country** list box. If so the **Currency Format** option should read "£1.22", as shown below.

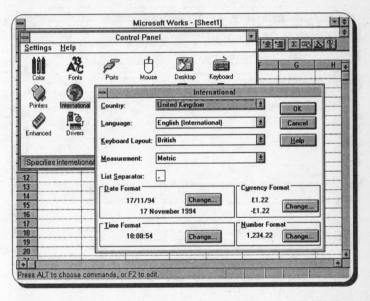

Now change the contents of cell A5 from 'Consult' to 'Consultancy'.

Saving a Worksheet

At this point, you might like to stop entering information in your worksheet, and save the work so far carried out, before leaving the program. You can do this by choosing the **File,**

Save command which reveals an appropriate dialogue box. In this box you are offered the default worksheet name SHEET1.WKS as a possible name for saving the file this very first time. Underneath this highlighted field is displayed a list of existing files in the current directory. You could select one of these if you wanted to overwrite its contents.

For our exercise, type the filename PROJECT1 (which will replace the default name and press <Enter> (the extension .WKS will be added by Works). If you prefer to save your work on a floppy disc in, say, the A: drive, you could make selections in the **Drives** and **Directories** boxes. Note that the worksheet name in the title bar changes from SHEET1 to PROJECT1 as soon as you press <Enter> and the file is saved on disc.

What you should see displayed on your screen after the above commands have been issued, is shown above.

At this point you could exit Works for Windows and switch off your computer in the knowledge that your work is saved on disc and can be retrieved at any time.

Exiting Works for Windows:

To exit Works, use the **File, Exit Works** command, or the <Alt+F4> keys. If you have made any changes to your work since the last time you saved it, an alert box will be displayed on your screen to ask you if you would like to save the file before leaving the program.

Filling in a Worksheet

We will use, as an example of how a spreadsheet can be built up, the few entries on 'Project Analysis' which we used previously. If you haven't saved the PROJECT1 example, don't worry as you could just as easily start afresh.

Retrieving a Worksheet:

If you have saved PROJECT1, then enter the Works program, and choose the **Open Existing File** icon from the Startup box. Works will display a dialogue box and ask you the name of the file to open with the default file name given as *.w*, in the first field of the dialogue box. In the second field, all the appropriate files are displayed. You can select the filename PROJECT1 either by clicking at its name, followed by clicking at the **OK** button, or by pressing <Alt+N> to move into the **File Name** box, pressing the <Tab> key to move down and then highlighting the required file before pressing <Enter>.

When the file is open, use the **F2** function key to 'Edit' the existing entries, or simply retype the contents of cells (see the next section for the formatting of the example) so that your worksheet looks like the one on the next page.

Formatting Entries:

Because of the length of some of the labels used and the formatting of the numbers, the default widths of cells in our worksheet were changed from the existing 10 to 12. If you haven't done this already, mark the cell block A1:E1, and choose the **Format, Column Width** command, and type 12 for the new width of the cells.

The information in cell A1

       PROJECT ANALYSIS: ADEPT CONSULTANTS LTD

was entered left justified and formatted by choosing the Courier, size 12, Italic Toolbar icons. The labels in the cell block B3-E3 were formatted with the Right Align icon, so they are displayed right justified.

The numbers within the cell block B5-E17 were formatted by clicking the Currency icon, which defaulted to two decimal places. All the labels appearing in column A (apart from that in cell A1) were just typed in (left justified), as shown.

The lines in cells A4 to E4 and A14 to E14 were entered using the **Format**, **Border** command and selecting **Top**. Those in cells A6 to E6 and A16 to E16 were entered using the **Format**, **Border** command and selecting **Bottom**.

Entering Text, Numbers and Formulae:

When text, numbers or formulae are entered into a cell, or reference is made to the contents of a cell by the cell address, or a Works for Windows function is entered into a cell, then the content of the message line changes from 'Press ALT to choose commands, or F2 to edit' to 'Press ENTER, or ESC to cancel'. This message can be changed back to the former one either by completing an entry and pressing <Enter> or one of the arrow keys, or by pressing the <Esc> key.

In our example, we can find the 1st quarter total income from consultancy, by activating cell E5 and typing the formula

```
=B5+C5+D5
```

followed by <Enter>. The total first quarter consultancy income is added, using this formula, and the result is placed in cell E5. Note, however, that when cell E5 is activated, the 'formula bar' displays the actual formula used to calculate the contents of the cell.

Complete the insertion into the spreadsheet of the various amounts under 'costs' and then choose the **File, Save As** command to save the resultant worksheet under the filename PROJECT2, before going on any further. Remember that saving your work on disc often is a good policy to get used to, as even the shortest power cut can cause the loss of hours of hard work!

Using Functions

In our example, writing a formula that adds the contents of three columns is not too difficult or lengthy a task. But imagine having to add 20 columns the same way! For this reason Works for Windows, like most spreadsheets, has an in-built summation function (for others see Appendix A) in the form of =SUM( ) which can be used to add any number of columns (or rows).

To illustrate how this function can be used, activate cell E5 and type

```
=SUM(
```

then use the arrow keys to move the highlighted cell to the start of the summation range (B5 in this case), then press colon (:) to anchor the starting point of the range, and use the arrow keys to move the cell pointer to the end of the summation range (in this case D5). What appears against the cell indicator is the entry

```
SUM(B5:D5
```

which has to be completed by typing the closing parenthesis (round bracket) and pressing <Enter>.

79

The Autosum Function:

Another very clever feature in Works for Windows is the facility to automatically enter the above =SUM() function into the worksheet. To automatically sum a series of numbers in either a column, or a row, place the active cell below the column, or to the right of the row, and click the Autosum Toolbar icon, shown here, or press the <Ctrl+M> quick key combination. Works enters the formula for you; all you have to do is press <Enter>, or click the Enter button (√) on the Formula bar, to accept it.

Copying Cell Contents:

To copy information into other cells we could repeat the above procedure (in this particular case entering the SUM() function in each cell within the cell range E8 through E13), or we could choose the **Edit**, **Copy** command, point to the cell we would like to copy information into and **Paste** it.

To illustrate the copy command, activate cell E5 and choose the **Edit**, **Copy** command, or press <Ctrl+C>, which copies the cell contents to the Windows clipboard. Move the highlighted cell to E8 and press **Edit**, **Paste**, or the <Ctrl+V> quick key. Then, block the cell range E8:E13 (by either using the <Shift+Down> keystroke or dragging the mouse) and choose the **Edit, Fill Down** command.

Immediately this command is chosen, its execution causes the actual sums of the 'relative' columns to appear on the target area. Notice that when we activate cell E5, the function target range is B5:D5, while when we activate cell E8 the function target range changes to B8:D8 which indicates that copying formulae with this method causes the 'relative' target range to be copied. Had the 'absolute' target range been copied instead, the result of the various summations would have been wrong.

Now complete the insertion of functions and formulae in the rest of the worksheet, noting that 'Total Costs' is the summation of rows 8 through 13, 'Profit' is the subtraction of 'Total Costs' from 'Consultancy', and that 'Cumulative' in row 19 refers to cumulative profit. Then add another column to your worksheet to calculate (and place in column F) the average monthly values of earnings, costs, and profit, using the =AVG( ) function. The worksheet, up to this point, should look like the one below. To make room on the screen for all 6 columns we changed the Font to Courier 10 points, but we could have used the **View**, **Zoom** feature instead. We also emboldened all the column and row titles.

	A	B	C	D	E	F
1	PROJECT ANALYSIS: ADEPT CONSULTANTS LTD					
2						
3		Jan	Feb	Mar	1st Quart	Average
4						
5	Consultancy	£14,000.00	£15,000.00	£16,000.00	£45,000.00	£15,000.00
6						
7	Costs:					
8	Wages	£2,000.00	£3,000.00	£4,000.00	£9,000.00	£3,000.00
9	Travel	£400.00	£500.00	£600.00	£1,500.00	£500.00
10	Rent	£300.00	£300.00	£300.00	£900.00	£300.00
11	Heat/Light	£150.00	£200.00	£150.00	£500.00	£166.67
12	Phone/Fax	£250.00	£300.00	£350.00	£900.00	£300.00
13	Adverts	£1,100.00	£1,200.00	£1,300.00	£3,600.00	£1,200.00
14						
15	Total Costs	£4,200.00	£5,500.00	£6,700.00	£16,400.00	£5,466.67
16						
17	Profit	£9,800.00	£9,500.00	£9,300.00	£28,600.00	£9,533.33
18						
19	Cumulative	£9,800.00	£19,300.00	£28,600.00		
20						

Erasing Cell Contents:

If you make any mistakes and copy information into cells you did not mean to, then choose the **Edit, Clear** command. To blank the contents within a range of adjacent cells, first select the cell block, then use the command.

Once you are satisfied that what appears on your screen is the same our example, use the **File Save As** command to save your worksheet under the filename PROJECT3, as we shall be using this example in the next chapter.

Quick Key Combinations

We have already discussed how you can move around a worksheet, edit information in a cell, or mark a range of cells using the pull-down sub-menus, or the Toolbar.

Another method of achieving these and other operations (some of which will be discussed in the next chapter) is by the use of quick key combinations, which do not require the menu bar to be activated. As you get used to the Works package, you might find it easier to use some of the quick key combinations which can save you a lot of time.

The following key combinations are some of those for use with the spreadsheet tool, for a fuller listing see Appendix B.

Moving and Selecting

Go To	F5
Move right one window	Ctrl+PgDn
Move left one window	Ctrl+PgUp
Move to next named range	Shift+F5
Move to next unlocked cell	Tab
Move to previous unlocked cell	Shift+Tab
Select worksheet row	Ctrl+F8
Select worksheet column	Shift+F8
Select whole worksheet	Ctrl+Shift+F8
Cancel a selection	Esc
Activate Autosum	Ctrl+M

Editing

Copy contents of cell above	Ctrl+' (apostrophe)
Calculate now	F9
View chart	Shift+F10
View worksheet	F10

Working in the formula bar

Activate/clear the formula bar	Backspace, or Del
Confirm information in a cell	Enter
Confirm a range of cells	Ctrl+Enter
Edit cell in formula bar	F2

Printing a Worksheet

To print a worksheet, make sure that the printer you propose to use was defined when you first installed Works. To check what was installed, choose the **File, Printer Setup** command. For further details on 'Printer Setup', 'Page Setup',

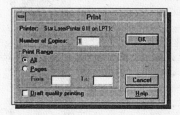

'Print Preview', and the use of 'Headers and Footers', please refer to Chapter 3. Once a printer has been selected, Works for Windows will continue to print to that printer from all the tools.

To print a worksheet, choose the **File, Print** command, or use the <Ctrl+P> quick key combination, both of which open the dialogue box, shown above.

 Clicking on the Print Toolbar icon will send to the printer without giving you a chance to check, or change, your settings, or what is sent.

Note that the default settings are 1 copy, **All** pages, and all text styles, etc., to print. You can change any of the options by choosing to print a different **Number of Copies**, selecting which pages to print, and setting **Draft quality printing** output, if you wish.

Before printing to paper, select the **File, Print Preview** command, or click the Print Preview Toolbar icon, shown here, to see how much of your worksheet will fit on your selected paper size. This depends very much on the chosen font. If the **Print Preview** option displays only part of your worksheet, and you then direct output to the printer, what does not fit on one page will be printed out on subsequent pages. To fit more of your worksheet on one page, you should reduce the selected font. Thus, the **Print Preview** option allows you to see the layout of the final printed page, which can save a few trees and, equally important to you, a lot of frustration and wear and tear on your printer.

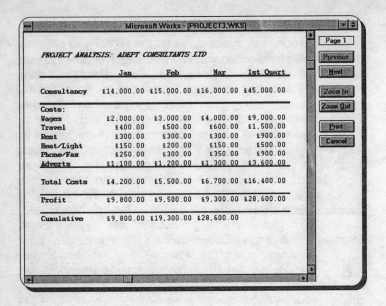

PROJECT ANALYSIS: ADEPT CONSULTANTS LTD

	Jan	Feb	Mar	1st Quart
Consultancy	£14,000.00	£15,000.00	£16,000.00	£45,000.00
Costs:				
Wages	£2,000.00	£3,000.00	£4,000.00	£9,000.00
Travel	£400.00	£500.00	£600.00	£1,500.00
Rent	£300.00	£300.00	£300.00	£900.00
Heat/Light	£150.00	£200.00	£150.00	£500.00
Phone/Fax	£250.00	£300.00	£350.00	£900.00
Adverts	£1,100.00	£1,200.00	£1,300.00	£3,600.00
Total Costs	£4,200.00	£5,500.00	£6,700.00	£16,400.00
Profit	£9,800.00	£9,500.00	£9,300.00	£28,600.00
Cumulative	£9,800.00	£19,300.00	£28,600.00	

Page 1
Previous
Next
Zoom In
Zoom Out
Print
Cancel

Setting a Print Area:

To select a smaller print area than the current worksheet, first block the required area, then choose the **Format**, **Set Print Area** command and press **OK**. You can then either preview the selected area, or print it on paper.

To reset the print area to the entire worksheet, choose the **Edit**, **Select All** command, then **Format**, **Set Print Area** once more, before attempting to either preview your worksheet or send it to the printer.

6. WORKSHEET SKILLS & GRAPHS

We will now use the worksheet saved under PROJECT3 (see end of previous chapter) to show how we can add to it, rearrange information in it and freeze titles in order to make entries easier, before going on to discuss more advanced topics. If you haven't saved PROJECT3 on disc, it will be necessary for you to enter the information into the Works for Windows spreadsheet so that you can benefit from what is to be introduced in this chapter. Having done this, save your work before going on with the suggested alterations. If you have saved PROJECT3, then choose the **File, Open Existing File** command and load the PROJECT3 file. On pressing **OK**, the worksheet is brought into the computer's memory and displayed on screen.

	A	B	C	D	E	F
				Microsoft Works - [PROJECT3.WKS]		
	File Edit View Insert Format Tools Window Help					
	Courier 10 B I U Σ					
	F15 =AVG(B15:D15)					
1	*PROJECT ANALYSIS: ADEPT CONSULTANTS LTD*					
2						
3		Jan	Feb	Mar	1st Quart	Average
4						
5	Consultancy	£14,000.00	£15,000.00	£16,000.00	£45,000.00	£15,000.00
6						
7	Costs:					
8	Wages	£2,000.00	£3,000.00	£4,000.00	£9,000.00	£3,000.00
9	Travel	£400.00	£500.00	£600.00	£1,500.00	£500.00
10	Rent	£300.00	£300.00	£300.00	£900.00	£300.00
11	Heat/Light	£150.00	£200.00	£150.00	£500.00	£166.67
12	Phone/Fax	£250.00	£300.00	£350.00	£900.00	£300.00
13	Adverts	£1,100.00	£1,200.00	£1,300.00	£3,600.00	£1,200.00
14						
15	Total Costs	£4,200.00	£5,500.00	£6,700.00	£16,400.00	£5,466.67
16						
17	Profit	£9,800.00	£9,500.00	£9,300.00	£28,600.00	£9,533.33
18						
19	Cumulative	£9,800.00	£19,300.00	£28,600.00		
20						

Press ALT to choose commands, or F2 to edit

The Spreadsheet Toolbar

As with the word processor tool, mouse lovers have an advantage when using the spreadsheet, in that they can make use of the Toolbar, some of whose options we have already discussed. The Toolbar occupies the third line down the **View**, **Toolbar** command. This is a toggle switch, when the '√' shows the Toolbar will display, otherwise it will not. The only advantage to be gained by not showing the Toolbar, is that you gain one line on your screen display.

To use the Toolbar you simply click the mouse on one of the icon buttons shown below, and the command selected will be effected on worksheet cells that are highlighted.

The meanings of the Toolbar options are as follows:

Option	*Result*
Courier	Specify a font type for the cells selected. Clicking the arrow (↓) will open the font list
12	Specify a font size for selected cells. Clicking the arrow (↓) will open the list of available sizes
	Open the Startup box, to open new or existing files
	Save the current document
	Print sheet, or range, using the current settings
	Print Preview
	Cut highlighted entry to the clipboard
	Copy to the clipboard
	Paste from clipboard
	Embolden highlighted entry
	Make highlighted entry italics
	Underline highlighted entry
	Left align highlighted cells
	Centre align highlighted cells
	Right align highlighted cells

Σ	Autosum a column, or row, of numbers
💰	Format selected cells as currency with 2 decimal places
📈	Create a chart using the selected entry data
❓	Activate help, Cue Cards, Tutorial or WorkWizards

Controlling Cell Contents

We will now add some more information to the worksheet with the insertion of another quarter's figures between columns E and F. In fact, we need to insert four columns altogether.

In general, you can insert or delete columns and rows in a worksheet, copy cell contents (including formulae) from one part of the worksheet to another and freeze titles in order to make entries into cells easier.

Inserting Rows & Columns:

To insert columns into a worksheet, point to the column heading where a column is to be inserted, in our case F, and press the left mouse button, which highlights the whole column. Then choose the **Insert**, **Row/Column** command. Had you highlighted a specific cell, say F1, choosing the **Insert**, **Row/Column** command would have opened a dialogue box, asking you to specify 'row' or 'column' insertion.

Repeat the insertion command three more times so that the column headed 'Average' appears in column J. To insert three columns in one operation, select the three columns to the right of where you want the insertion before you choose the **Insert**, **Row/Column** command. We could now start entering information into the empty columns, but if we did this we would then have to re-enter all the formulae used to calculate the various results for the first quarter.

An alternative, much easier, way is to copy everything from the first quarter to the second and then only edit the actual numeric information within the various columns. We will choose this second method to achieve our goal. First, highlight the cell block B3:E19, move the highlighter to the top border of the block where it will change to a DRAG pointer. Hold down the <Ctrl> key and Drag copy the block four columns to the right, as shown below.

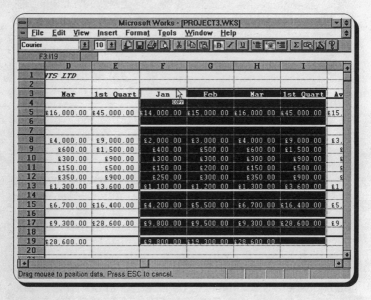

If necessary, use the **Format, Column Width** command, to change the width of any cells from 10 characters to 12. Now the widths of the highlighted columns are suitably adjusted, edit the copied headings 'Jan', 'Feb', 'Mar', and '1st Quart' to 'Apr', 'May', 'Jun', and '2nd Quart'. Save the resultant work under the filename PROJECT4 (don't forget to use the **Save As** command)!

Freezing Titles:
Note that by the time the highlighted bar is moved to column J, the 'titles' in column A have scrolled to the left and are outside the viewing area of the screen. This will make editing of numeric information very difficult if we can't see what refers to what. Therefore, before we attempt any further editing, it would be a good idea to use the 'Titles' command to freeze the titles in column A and rows 1 to 3.

To freeze column (or row) headings on a worksheet, move the highlighted bar to the cell below the column (or to the right of the row) you wish to freeze on the screen (in our case B4), and select the **Format**, **Freeze Titles** toggle command.

On execution, the headings on the chosen column (and row) are frozen but the highlighter can still be moved into the frozen area. Moving around the worksheet, leaves the headings in these columns (and/or rows) frozen on the screen. Carry this out and change the numbers in the worksheet cells F5 to H13 to those below.

	A	F	G	H	I	J
				Microsoft Works - [PROJECT4.WKS]		
	File **Edit** **View** **Insert** **Format** **Tools** **Window** **Help**					
	Courier	10				
	J5	=AVG(B5:D5)				
1	*PROJECT ANAL*					
2						
3		Apr	May	Jun	2nd Quart	Average
4						
5	Consultancy	£15,500.00	£16,000.00	£16,500.00	£48,000.00	£15,000.00
6						
7	Costs:					
8	Wages	£3,500.00	£4,000.00	£4,500.00	£12,000.00	£3,000.00
9	Travel	£500.00	£550.00	£580.00	£1,630.00	£500.00
10	Rent	£300.00	£300.00	£300.00	£900.00	£300.00
11	Heat/Light	£150.00	£120.00	£100.00	£370.00	£166.67
12	Phone/Fax	£300.00	£350.00	£400.00	£1,050.00	£300.00
13	Adverts	£1,250.00	£1,300.00	£1,350.00	£3,900.00	£1,200.00
14						
15	Total Costs	£6,000.00	£6,620.00	£7,230.00	£19,850.00	£5,466.67
16						
17	Profit	£9,500.00	£9,380.00	£9,270.00	£28,150.00	£9,533.33
18						
19	Cumulative	£9,500.00	£18,880.00	£28,150.00		
20						

Press ALT to choose commands, or F2 to edit.

Save the file again, but this time use the Save Toolbar icon, to keep the name PROJECT4.

Note: If you examine this worksheet carefully, you will notice that two errors have occurred; one of these has to do with the average calculation in column J, while the other has to do with the accumulated values in the second quarter.

89

Non-Contiguous Address Range:

The calculations of average values in column J of the above worksheet are wrong because the range values in the formula are still those entered for the first quarter only.

To correct these, highlight cell J5 and press **F2** to edit the formula displayed in the formula bar from =AVG(B5:D5) to

```
=AVG(B5:D5,F5:H5)
```

which on pressing <Enter> changes the value shown in cell J5. Note the way the argument of the function is written when non-contiguous address ranges are involved. Here we have two such address ranges, B5:D5 and F5:H5, which we separate with a comma.

Now replicate the formula to the J8:J13 cell range by highlighting cell J5, choosing the **Edit, Copy** command, or <Ctrl+C>, move the highlight to cell J8 and use **Edit, Paste**. Then drag the highlight from J8 to J13 (to select the range) and choose the **Edit, Fill Down** command. Finally, repeat the **Paste** operation for the target cells J15 and J17.

You could also do all these actions with the Copy and Paste icons. The choice is yours!

Relative and Absolute Cell Addresses:

Entering a mathematical expression into Works, such as the formula in cell C19 which was

```
=B19+C17
```

causes Works to interpret it as 'add the contents of cell one column to the left of the current position, to the contents of cell two rows above the current position'. In this way, when the formula was later replicated into cell address D19, the contents of the cell relative to the left position of D19 (i.e. C19) and the contents of the cell two rows above it (i.e. D17) were used, instead of the original cell addresses entered in C19. This is relative addressing.

To see the effect of relative versus absolute addressing, type in cell E19 the formula

```
=E5-E15
```

which will be interpreted as relative addressing. Now, add another row to your worksheet, namely 'Profit/Quart' in row 21, and copy the formula in cell E19 to cell E21, using the **Edit Copy** command. The displayed calculated value in E21 is, of course, wrong (negative) because the cell references in the copied formula are now given as

```
=E7-E17
```

as the references were copied relatively.

Now change the formula in E19 by editing it to

```
=$E$5-$E$15
```

which is interpreted as absolute addressing. Copying this formula into cell E21 calculates the correct result. Highlight cell E21 and observe the cell references in its formula; they have not changed from those of cell E19.

The $ sign must prefix both the column reference and the row reference. Mixed cell addressing is permitted; as for example when a column address reference is needed to be taken as absolute, while a row address reference is needed

Microsoft Works - [PROJECT5.WKS]						
File Edit View Insert Format Tools Window Help						
21	=$E$19+$I$17					
	A	F	G	H	I	J
1		*PROJECT ANALYSIS: ADEPT CONSULTANTS LTD*				
2						
3		Apr	May	Jun	2nd Quart	Average
4						
5	Consultancy	£15,500.00	£16,000.00	£16,500.00	£48,000.00	£15,500.00
6						
7	Costs:					
8	Wages	£3,500.00	£4,000.00	£4,500.00	£12,000.00	£3,500.00
9	Travel	£500.00	£550.00	£580.00	£1,630.00	£521.67
10	Rent	£300.00	£300.00	£300.00	£900.00	£300.00
11	Heat/Light	£150.00	£120.00	£100.00	£370.00	£145.00
12	Phone/Fax	£300.00	£350.00	£400.00	£1,050.00	£325.00
13	Adverts	£1,250.00	£1,300.00	£1,350.00	£3,900.00	£1,250.00
14						
15	Total Costs	£6,000.00	£6,620.00	£7,230.00	£19,850.00	£6,041.67
16						
17	Profit	£9,500.00	£9,380.00	£9,270.00	£28,150.00	£9,458.33
18						
19	Cumulative	£9,500.00	£18,880.00	£28,150.00	£56,750.00	
20						
21	Profit/Quart				£56,750.00	
22						

Press ALT to choose commands, or F2 to edit.

91

to be taken as relative. In such a case, only the column letter is prefixed by the $ sign.

Finally, correct the formulae in cells I19 and I21 (they should both contain '=$E$19+$I$17') in order to obtain the results shown on the previous page.

Moving Cell Contents:

To improve the printed output of PROJECT4, we could move the caption to somewhere in the middle of the worksheet. Since the cell whose contents we propose to move is frozen, the move command has to be preceded by additional keystrokes. From the keyboard, first unfreeze the title with the **Format**, **Freeze Titles** command. Now, highlight cell A1 and choose the **Edit, Cut** command (or <Ctrl+X>), which removes the cell contents from the worksheet and places them on the Windows clipboard, then highlight cell F1 and **Paste** the clipboard's contents. Save the resultant worksheet under the filename PROJECT5.

Some New Features

Version 3.0 of Works for Windows includes several new spreadsheet features worth briefly mentioning.

Alignment:

Another method of carrying out the title formatting in the last example would be to use the new ability to centre a cell's contents within a selected range with the **Format**, **Alignment**, **Center across selection** command.

Some other new features in this dialogue box are the vertical alignment options and the ability to **Wrap Text** (but not numbers or formulae) within a cell. You can now have several lines of text in the same cell.

Automatic Column Widths:

Choosing the **Best Fit** check box in the **Format**, **Column Width** dialogue box lets Works determine the best column width to accommodate all the entries in selected columns, or parts of columns. You could use this after selecting the whole sheet and not have to worry about cell widths again.

Inserting Functions:

You can now automatically choose a function with the **Insert**, **Function** command and Works inserts it, including its arguments, into the formula bar. This feature saves you having to remember all the available function names, and from looking up the argument details every time.

The UNDO Command:

The **Edit**, **Undo** command reverses certain commands, or deletes the last entry you typed, but only if it used straight away, otherwise 'Cannot Undo' appears greyed on the **Edit** menu if you cannot undo the previous action. Immediately after you undo an action, this command changes to **Redo**, which allows you to reverse the action.

Automatic Cell Fill:

A useful feature which could save you much typing is the **Edit**, **Fill Series** command, which fills highlighted cells with a series of numbers or dates. You type the first entry, highlight the cells to fill and use this command to quickly enter the rest of a series of consecutive dates or numbers in the column or row.

Try typing 'Jan' in a heading cell, highlight the next eleven cells to the right, use the **Edit**, **Fill Series** command, select **Month**, and see what happens. Computers are supposed to make things easier after all!

Cell Formatting Options:

The **Format**, **Patterns** command gives you control over the pattern and colour of the shading of highlighted cells. To change the colour of a cell's contents you must use the **Format**, **Font and Style**, **Color** option.

The new **Format**, **AutoFormat** option gives a series of built-in formats you can apply to any highlighted range to give it a more 'professional' appearance.

The format options offered are combinations of number formats, alignments, fonts, borders, patterns and shading, column widths and row heights. Try them, you might find some are usable.

Adding Spreadsheet Charts

Works for Windows allows you to represent information in graphical form which makes data more accessible to non-expert users who might not be familiar with the spreadsheet format. In any case, the well known saying 'a picture is worth a thousand words', applies equally well to charts and figures.

You use the charting facility of Works for Windows by first selecting a data range to be charted on your worksheet, such as A8:D10 on our file PROJECT5, and then choosing the **Tools**, **Create New Chart** command, or pressing the New Chart Toolbar icon. This opens the New Chart box, shown here. To see what types of chart, or graphs, are available scroll through the **What type of chart do you want?** list box. An example of each, based on the selected spreadsheet data, is shown in the box.

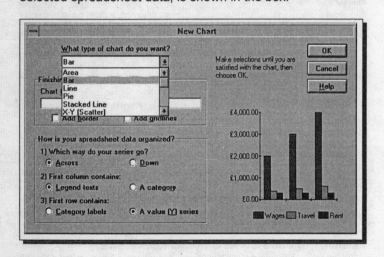

Although Works for Windows has eight main two-dimensional, and four three-dimensional, chart and graph types, there are many optional ways to view each type, and they can be grouped and overlapped, which allows you to add considerably to the list. The different chart-types can be selected from the box above, or the menu, or the new Toolbar, when you are in a charting window.

94

To enhance your charts you can add titles, legends, labels, and can select grids, fill types, scaling, fonts, etc. These charts (you can have several per spreadsheet) can be displayed on the screen and can be sent to an appropriate output device, such as a plotter or printer.

The main graph types available are listed below, with their Charting Toolbar icons, where available. They are normally used for the following relationships between data:

Area

for comparing value changes to the total over a period of time. 2-D or 3-D options available.

Bar

for comparing differences in data over a period of time. Displays the values of dependent variables as vertical columns. The stacked and 100% options, show relationships to the whole. 2-D or 3-D options available.

Line

for representing data values with points joined by lines and appearing at equal intervals along the x-axis. For such charts, the x-axis could be intervals in time, such as labels representing months. 2-D or 3-D options available.

Pie

for comparing parts with the whole. Displays data blocks as slices of a pie. Can contain only one series. 2-D or 3-D options available.

Stacked Line

for representing the total in each category. A line chart in which the lines are stacked.

XY (Scatter)

for showing the relationship, or degree of relationship, between numeric values in different groups of data. Used for finding patterns or trends in data (whether variables are dependent on or affect one another).

Radar

for showing changes in data relative to a centre point and to other data. Useful for relative comparisons.

Combination

for displaying related data measured in different units; used for comparing two different kinds of data or to show a correlation that might be difficult to recognise.

Charts can be displayed on the screen at the same time as the worksheet, but in a separate window. As charts are dynamic, any changes made to the data are automatically reflected on the defined charts.

Preparing for a Bar Chart:

In order to illustrate some of the graphing capabilities of Works for Windows, we will now plot an income from consultancies graph of the PROJECT5 file.

First we need to define what we want to chart. However, the specified range of data to be charted must be contiguous for each chart. But, in our example, the range of data is split into two areas; Jan-Mar (occupying cell positions B3:D3), and Apr-Jun (occupying cell positions F3:H3), with the corresponding income values in cells B5:D5 and F5:H5. Thus, to create an appropriate contiguous data range, we must first replicate the labels and values of these two range areas in another area of the spreadsheet (say, beginning in cell B23 for the actual month labels and B24 for the values of the corresponding income), as shown on the next page.

To do this, use the **Edit, Copy** and **Paste** commands to copy the labels in the above two cell-ranges into the target area. However, before you replicate the cells containing numeric values, consider what might happen if these cells

File Edit View Insert Format Tools Window Help

Courier   12

H24

	A	B	C	D	E	F	G
1					PROJECT ANALYSIS: ADEPT CONSULTANTS LTD		
2							
3		Jan	Feb	Mar	1st Quart	Apr	May
4							
5	Consultancy	£14,000.00	£15,000.00	£16,000.00	£45,000.00	£15,500.00	£16,000.00
6							
7	Costs:						
8	Wages	£2,000.00	£3,000.00	£4,000.00	£9,000.00	£3,500.00	£4,000.00
9	Travel	£400.00	£500.00	£600.00	£1,500.00	£500.00	£550.00
10	Rent	£300.00	£300.00	£300.00	£900.00	£300.00	£300.00
11	Heat/Light	£150.00	£200.00	£150.00	£500.00	£150.00	£120.00
12	Phone/Fax	£250.00	£300.00	£350.00	£900.00	£300.00	£350.00
13	Adverts	£1,100.00	£1,200.00	£1,300.00	£3,600.00	£1,250.00	£1,300.00
14							
15	Total Costs	£4,200.00	£5,500.00	£6,700.00	£16,400.00	£6,000.00	£6,620.00
16							
17	Profit	£9,800.00	£9,500.00	£9,300.00	£28,600.00	£9,500.00	£9,380.00
18							
19	Cumulative	£9,800.00	£19,300.00	£28,600.00	£28,600.00	£9,500.00	£18,880.00
20							
21	Profit/Quart				£28,600.00		
22							
23	Months	Jan	Feb	Mar	Apr	May	Jun
24	Income	£14,000.00	£15,000.00	£16,000.00	£15,500.00	£16,000.00	£16,500.00
25							

contain formulae, and you used the **Edit, Paste** command to replicate them. Using this command would cause the relative cell addresses to adjust to the new locations and each formula will then recalculate a new value for each cell which will give wrong results.

The Paste Special Command:

The **Edit, Paste Special** command allows you to copy only cell references without adjusting to the new location. To do this, mark the cell range to be copied (in this case B5:D5) and choose the **Edit, Copy** command, move the highlighter to cell B24 and press **Edit, Paste Special**, select the **Values only** option from the displayed dialogue box and press <Enter>, or select **OK**. Now repeat the same procedure for the values under Apr-Jun, but copy them into E24 to form a contiguous data range.

Finally, add labels for 'Months' and 'Income' in cells A23 and A24, respectively, as shown above.

The Chart Editor

To obtain a chart of 'Income' versus 'Months', block cell range A23:G24 and choose the **Tools**, **Create New Chart** command, or the New Chart Toolbar icon. Select **OK** to accept the default Bar chart type and Works for Windows clears the screen and draws a bar chart of the information contained in the blocked range of cells. This places you in 'Charting' mode and in a separate window. A new set of menu commands and a new Toolbar are available, as shown.

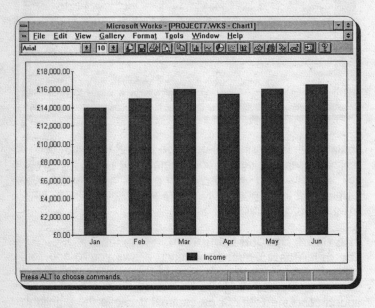

The chart is displayed in its own window, so to return to the worksheet you can press the <Ctrl+F6> keys, or use the **Window** menu options. Choosing **View**, **Chart** again, reveals that the chart just displayed on screen appears under the name **Chart1** in the list box. To select a different type chart, you must return to Chart mode by selecting a Chart window. You can then choose the **Gallery** menu command which reveals a sub-menu with all the available chart types. Note that the **Bar** type has a tick against it indicating Chart1's type.

You could select another type from the displayed list, but if you do your Bar chart will not be saved.

To select another type of chart, but still retain the first one, activate the **Tools**, **Create New Chart** command, which makes a copy of the current chart as **Chart2** and displays it. Use the **Gallery** command and choose the **Line** option, which offers the choice of 6 types of line graphs, as shown here.

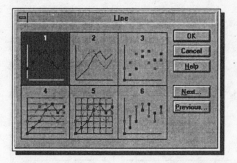

If you need a more detailed (and more colourful) description of these options we suggest that you use the **Help** button from this box. Pressing the **<<** and **>>** buttons below the Help menu bar will step you through complete details of all the available chart types. When satisfied, press <Alt+F4> to return to the Chart window.

Before making a selection from the Line box, look at the icons located on the Toolbar. The Line icon should be 'depressed'. Now press the **Next** button, which opens the Pie dialogue box and, in turn, depresses the Pie icon on the Toolbar. Use the **Next** and **Previous** buttons to view all of the available chart options and, at the same time, note the meanings of the icons on the Toolbar.

When you return to the line dialogue box, select the default option '**1**', by double-clicking on its button. This will produce a line chart similar to the one on the next page.

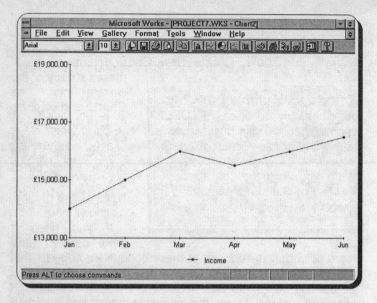

The shape of this line chart was improved by choosing the **Format**, **Vertical (Y) Axis** command and typing

```
13000
```

in the **Minimum** box.

There are a lot of other options that you can specify when creating a chart. Some of these are self evident, like titles, legends, data labels, and the inclusion of axis labels and grid lines. These will be discussed only if needed in the examples that follow.

Saving Charts:

Charts are saved with a spreadsheet when you save the spreadsheet to disc. Thus, saving the spreadsheet under the filename PROJECT7, will ensure that your charts are also saved under the same name. Since each chart is linked to the spreadsheet from which it was derived, if information on the spreadsheet changes, the charts associated with it will also change automatically.

Customising a Chart

In order to customise a chart, you need to know how to add titles and axis labels, how to change text fonts, the colour and pattern of the chart, and how to incorporate grid lines.

Drawing a Multiple Bar Chart:

As an exercise, open PROJECT7, if it is not already in memory, so we can build a new bar-type chart which deals with the monthly 'Costs' of Adept Consultants. As there are six different non-contiguous sets of costs, you must first copy them (including the cost description labels) using the **Edit, Paste Special** command, into a contiguous range below the 'Income' range (starting, say, at cell A27), as shown below.

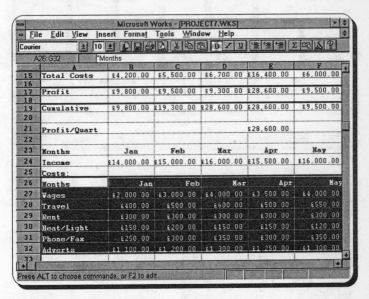

Having done this, copy the 'Months' labels from row 23 to row 26 and save the resultant worksheet under the filename PROJECT8.

Now block the cell range A26:G32, as shown, choose the **Tools**, **Create New Chart** command, type 'ADEPT CONSULTANTS' in the **Chart title** field and press **OK**.

Immediately this is done, the bar chart of the 6 different monthly costs is drawn automatically with each month in a different colour. The diagram below shows the result, after using the **View**, **Display as Printed** command.

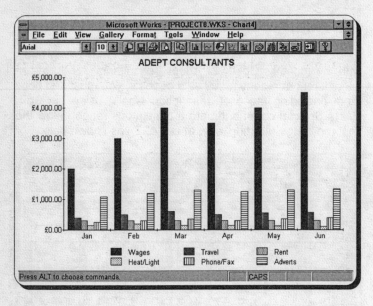

Chart Titles, Fonts & Sizes:

To add, or edit, a chart title, choose the **Edit**, **Titles** command which causes this dialogue box to be displayed on

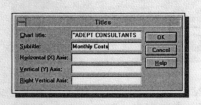

your screen. Type 'Monthly Costs' in the **Subtitle** field of the dialogue box and select **OK**.

To change the font and size of the newly created title, first action the **Edit**, **Select Title Text** command and then **Format**, **Font and Style** to display the 'Font and Style for Title' dialogue box. From this you can choose any of the fonts available to Works for Windows, set a new size by selecting from the list of sizes (given in points), change the colour and set other attributes.

To change the font of the subtitle and other text and numbers in a chart, choose **Format**, **Font and Style** without first selecting the Title.

The fonts and sizes of the text in the chart below were set as follows:

Chart title: Bodini Book, bold and italic, size 16
Other text & numbers: Bodini Book, size 8

Grid lines were added by selecting the **Format**, **Vertical (Y) Axis** command and activating the **Show Gridlines** option.

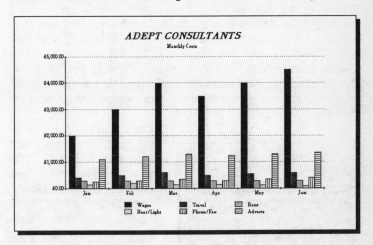

Printing a Chart:

Before printing, or previewing a chart, you should check your page settings with the **File**, **Page Setup** command. This opens a dialogue box similar to that shown on page 48, but with the following extra **Size** choices in the **Other Options** section.

Screen size - prints the chart the same size as it appears on the screen.

Full page, keep proportions - prints charts so that they use the full paper width (between the margins), but scales the vertical size to keep the chart in proportion.

Full page - the default option, stretches the chart to take up the full page (between all four margins). This can produce some weird charts with portrait paper setting.

Before printing a chart it is wise to always Preview it, from the Toolbar icon. You may find that you have to adjust your text font settings to get all the chart text to display. When you are satisfied, press **Print** to record your chart on paper, or **Cancel**, to return to the chart window.

Drawing a Pie Chart:

As a second example in chart drawing, use the 'Average' values of the costs from the worksheet of PROJECT9 to plot a pie chart. Select the range J8:J13 and again, use the **Tools**, **Create New Chart** command, followed by **OK**. Click the Pie Chart icon to open the 'Pie' dialogue box and double click your mouse on the **6** option. Your range should now be displayed in a colourful pie chart.

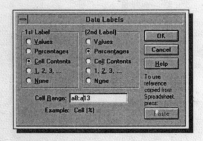

The labels on each segment are not very self explanatory though. To remedy this, use the **Edit**, **Data labels** command and type A8:A13 in the **Cell Range** text box as shown here. Select **OK** to leave the box and return to your chart.

Add an appropriate title to the chart and allocate a font and size to it as described previously. Your chart should now look something like that shown on the next page.

To explode one of the segments of the pie chart, choose the **Format**, **Patterns and Colors** command and select the number of the slice you would like to appear detached, from the displayed dialogue box. Slices, in this case, are numbered from 1 to 6 and are allocated to the pie chart in a clockwise direction. Thus, to explode the 'Rent' slice, select **3** in the **Slices** box, then activate the **Explode Slice** option and press the **Format** and **Close** buttons. In this way, you can emphasise one or more portions of the chart.

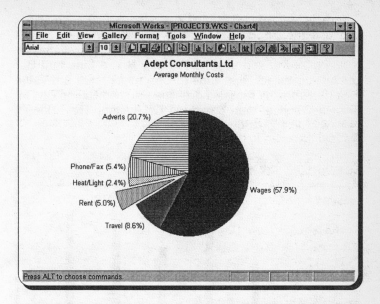

To cancel an 'exploded' selection, use the **Format**, **Patterns and Colors** command and press the **Format All** and **Close** buttons. Selecting other slices for exploding, without first cancelling previous selections, adds to the selection.

Mixing Chart Types:

To illustrate a combination of a bar and line chart, we will consider the variable monthly costs of Adept Consultants. This requires us to delete row 29 (the 'Rent' cost, which is fixed) from the worksheet. Just as well, since Works for Windows can only deal with a maximum of six categories and we would like to introduce average monthly costs as our sixth category.

Use the **Edit** command to delete the row dealing with 'Rent' from your worksheet, then create a new category in the renumbered row 32, to hold the average variable monthly costs. We will leave it to you to work out and place the cell formulae for this operation. If you have worked your way to here, this should not be too much of a problem.

To create a mixed chart, first mark the A26:G32 cell block and use the **Tools**, **Create New Chart** command, select Combination and press **OK**. The chart first displayed may be a little mixed up, so use the **Format**, **Mixed Line and Bar** command, select the **Line L** option for the **6th Value Y-Series** from the revealed dialogue box, and **Bar** options for the other series, then press the **OK** button. The following chart should appear on the screen.

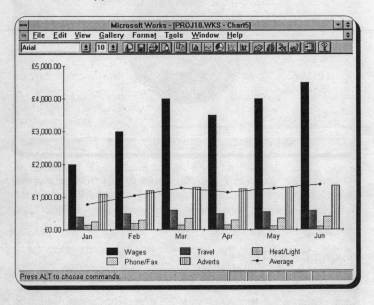

It is possible to display data using two y-axes, by using two different chart types; one type is then displayed on the left y-axis and another type is displayed on the right y-axis. The same thing can also be applied to two sub-groups of the same chart type. To do this, use the **Format**, **Two Vertical (Y) Axes** command and specify on the revealed dialogue box which series you want to appear on the left axis and which on the right axis.

Now you have scratched the surface of spreadsheet and charting useage, we hope you will continue to explore the other features we were unable to fit in.

7. THE DATABASE TOOL

A Works for Windows database is a file which contains related information, such as 'Customer's Names', 'Consultancy Details', 'Invoice No.', etc. A phone book is a simple database, stored on paper. In Works for Windows each record is entered as a worksheet row, with the fields of each record occupying corresponding columns.

The next section deals with the basic concepts of using a database, along with the database 'jargon' that is used in this book. If you are not familiar with database terminology then you should read this section first.

A database is a collection of data that exists, and is organised around a specific theme, or requirement. A database is used for storing information, so that it is quickly accessible. In the case of Works for Windows, data is stored in **data-files** which are specially structured files that reside on disc like other disc-files. To make accessing the data easier, each row or **record** of data within a database is structured in the same fashion, i.e., each record will have the same number of columns, or **fields**.

We define a database and its various elements as follows:

Database	A collection of data organised for a specific theme.
Data-file	Disc-file in which data is stored.
Record	A row of information relating to a single entry and comprising one or more fields.
Field	A single column of information of the same type, such as people's names.
Form	A screen in which one record of data can be entered, displayed, or edited.
List	The whole database displayed in a spreadsheet-like format. Multiple records can be entered and edited.
Query	A set of instructions to search the database for records with specific properties.

107

A good example of a database is a telephone directory. To cover the whole country many directories are needed, just as a database can comprise a number of data-files. The following shows how data is presented in such a directory.

```
Prowse H.B., 91 Cabot Close  .........................  Truro 76455
Pruce T.A., 15 Woodburn Road  ................  Plymouth 223248
Pryce C.W., 42 North Gate Road  ...............  St Austell 851662
Pryor A., 38 Western Approach  .................  Plymouth 238742
Pryor B.E., 79 Trevithick Road  .......................  Truro 74231
Queen S.R., 4 Ruskin Crescent  ...............  Camborne 712212
```

Information is structured in fields which are identified below, for a single record, as follows:

Name	Address	Town	Tel No.
Pryor B.E.	79 Trevithick Road	Truro	742310

Creating a Database

A database file, in Works for Windows, is created with the **File, Create a New File** command and then selecting **Database**. This produces an almost empty screen, with its own menu and Toolbar (see end of Chapter), and the database file DATA1.WDB is opened as a default. You should not forget to change its name when you save it. All database files are automatically given the extension .WDB when they are saved.

Database Screens:

This opening screen is a 'Form' window, or view, as shown on page 111. On it, as an example, we will build a 'front end' form to enter, and access, our data.

The other way of looking at, and accessing, a Works for Windows database is through the 'List' screen, as shown next.

File   Edit   View   Insert   Format   Tools   Window   Help

Times New Roman   10

Vibration Tests

	Customer Name	Details	Inv.No	Issued	Paid	O/D	Total
1	VORTEX Co. Ltd	Wind Tunnel Tests	8901	04/08/94	0		£120.84
2	AVON Construction	Adhesive Tests	8902	11/08/94	1		£103.52
3	BARROWS Associates	Tunnel Design Tests	8903	13/08/94	0		£99.32
4	STONEAGE Ltd	Carbon Dating Tests	8904	15/08/94	0		£55.98
5	PARKWAY Gravel	Material Size Tests	8905	20/08/94	0		£180.22
6	WESTWOOD Ltd	Load Bearing Tests	8906	20/08/94	0		£68.52
7	GLOWORM Ltd	Luminescence Tests	8907	20/08/94	0		£111.55
8	SILVERSMITH Co	X-Ray Diffract. Test	8908	20/08/94	1		£123.45
9	WORMGLAZE Ltd	Heat Transfer Tests	8909	29/08/94	0		£35.87
10	EALING Engines Dgn	Vibration Tests	8910	02/09/94	0		£58.95
11	HIRE Service Equip	Network Implement/n	8911	10/09/94	0		£290.00
12	EUROBASE Co. Ltd	Proj. Contr. Manag.	8912	18/09/94	0		£150.00
13	FREEMARKET Dealers	Stock Control Pack	8913	25/09/94	0		£560.00
14	OILRIG Construct.	Metal Fatigue Tests	8914	03/10/94	0		£96.63
15	TIME & Motion Ltd	Systems Analysis	8915	13/10/94	0		£120.35
16							
17							
18							
19							

Press ALT to choose commands, or F2 to edit.   10   15/15

The above shows the records of a simple database, suitable
for keeping track of the invoices issued by a small
engineering consulting company. As an example we will go
through the stages of setting up this database with the Works
for Windows package.

As previously mentioned, when a database file is opened,
the Form window is shown on the screen. Press **F9**, or the
List View Toolbar icon show here, or choose **View,
List,** to switch to an empty List screen. This gives a
spreadsheet type view of the database, with the
numbers down the left hand side referring to individual
records, and the column headings referring to the database
fields. The status line, at the bottom, shows which record the
cursor is in, how many records are currently displayed, and
how many are in the database.

The screen shown on the next page is of useful descriptive
information which is part of the Help system's Database
Overview, this is well worth viewing.

Use **F9**, or the Form View Toolbar icon shown, or the
View, **Form** command, to change back to the Form
window. We will use this window to build a suitable
entry form for our database. As it is a multi-page

Works for Windows Help

File　Edit　Bookmark　Help

Contents　Search　Back　History　<<　>>

Database overview

There are two ways to work with your database information:

■ In form view, you work with one record at a time on a customized form you create, such as an invoice or statement.

Underwater Photo Safari Tour Customers ─── Label

Last Name: Appleton　　Customer ID #: 111586N658
First Name: Edith
Street: 22381 42 Ave NE
City: Kirkland　State: WA
Zip: 38034
Tour: Cozumel

Field name
Field entry

■ In list view, you work with many records at once in a list, similar to a spreadsheet.

	First Name	Street	Field name
1	Edith	22381 42 Ave NE	Field entry
2			
3			

Field

In addition, you can use query view to select a particular group of records, and report definition view to

---

window, the co-ordinate information on the line below the Toolbar is needed to keep track of the current cursor position. This gives X and Y co-ordinates in the current system dimension units, (measured from the top left hand corner of each printed page). The page number of the current cursor position is shown on the Status Bar. The overall maximum form dimensions can be 3 pages long by 3 screens wide. A form can contain up to 256 database fields, as well as titles, labels and other text. Each field can hold up to 256 characters. A database can contain up to 32,000 records, which should be enough for most people!

Creating a Form

Move the cursor, either with the mouse, or the arrow keys, to the approximate screen location (7.0cm, 6.0cm), and type

```
Customer Name:
```

Make sure you do not omit the colon. Press <Enter>, select a width of 20 characters, and a height of 1 line, in the dialogue box. A dotted line is produced, showing the field location to the right of the field name, and the cursor is moved down to the next line.

Enter the remaining fields as shown in the table below.

Field Name	Width
Details:	20
Inv.No:	6
Issued:	10
Paid:	4
O/D:	5
Total:	10

You should now have a basic database entry form which looks something like the one shown below.

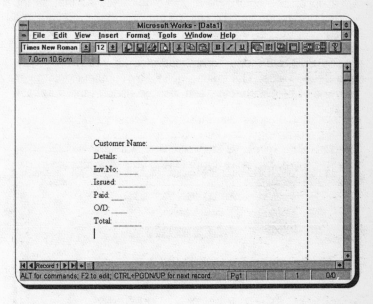

If you press the **F9** key, or the List View icon, you will see that the List screen now has a row of field titles along the top, above the working area. All of the titles are not, at the moment, completely visible, as the default column width for a List screen is 10, and some of the fields are longer than that.

These widths can be altered, so place the cursor in the top left cell of the screen, choose the **Format, Field Width** command, type **20** in the box and press <Enter>.

The List screen field widths are in fact independent of those chosen for the Form screen. In our example, we want them to be the same, so alter the other widths as well and then return to the form screen.

Form Editing:

Before entering any records, the entry form would benefit from some cosmetic attention. Place the cursor in the field title 'Details:' and click to select it. The mouse pointer changes and lets you drag an outline of the field around the screen. Move the field to the right until the top two fields are lined up on the colon. Move the other fields so that all the colons are in one vertical line, or until you have a layout you prefer. With the Drag and Drop function you simply select a field with your mouse pointer and drag it to a new position.

The **Edit** sub-menu commands also let you move, copy, and delete fields. The editing quick key combinations, given at the end of the chapter, can also be used in the database section.

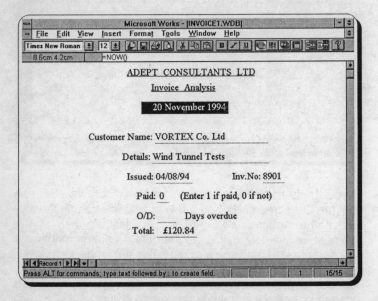

Place the cursor on the second screen line, at about the position (8.0cm, 1.0cm), type the database title

ADEPT CONSULTANTS LTD

and press <Enter>. As there was no colon at the end of the entered text, Works accepts it as a label, not a field. Labels can be placed in any unused space on the form screen. As the title is still highlighted it is a good time to carry out any enhancements. Click on the Underline Toolbar icon and then enter the other labels shown in the facing diagram.

Hiding a Field Name:
The 'date' cell, shown in our example as 20 November 1994, is not a label. It actually has a dotted line below it and is, in fact, a database field (called Date:), containing a formula to generate the current date, but with its field name switched off.

Place the cursor in the fifth line down, and create a 'Date:' field 20 characters wide. For the moment we will leave this cell empty. To hide it, highlight its field name, and choose the **Format, Show Field Name** command. The field name 'Date:' should now be turned off. If you wanted, you could now place a different label on top of it. This technique is useful if you want to keep actual field names short, but need longer descriptive ones on the front-end form, as could have been used with the 'O/D:' field (Overdue), shown in our example.

Entering Data in a Form
We will now enter the first record into the database. Your cursor should be in the date cell. Press <Tab> to move to the 'Customer Name:' field, and type:

Vortex Co. Ltd	press <Tab> and type,
Wind Tunnel Tests	press <Tab> and type,
4/8/94	press <Tab> and type,
8901	press <Tab> and type,
0	press <Tab> twice, and type,
120.84	press <Tab>

Nothing should have been entered in the 'O/D:' field. The last <Tab> should have completed the entry of record 1, and brought up an empty form for the next record. Press

<Ctrl+PgUp>, to move back one record, to the date cell of record 1.

When moving about a form, <Tab> and <Shift+Tab>, move the cursor between fields, whereas <Ctrl+PgUp> and <Ctrl+PgDn>, move between adjacent records.

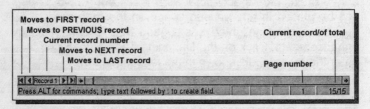

The arrow buttons on the left end of the Horizontal Scroll Bar can also be used to step through the records of a database, as is shown above.

Using Formulae in a Field:

Database formulae have two main applications; to automatically force the same entry in each similar field of every record in the database, or to calculate the contents of one field based on those of another. Each database field can only contain one formula. Once it is entered in the field of one record, it is automatically entered into all the other records. As in the spreadsheet, a formula must always be preceded by an equal sign (=).

In our database example we will enter formulae in two fields, the date formula next, and one that calculates the contents of a field, a little later on. With the cursor in the date cell, type

    =NOW ( )

As with the spreadsheet, this formula is shown on the screen, both in the cell and in the formula bar at the top of the screen. When you press <Enter>, a long number should appear in the date cell, but the formula will still be shown in the formula bar. It generates the number of days since the beginning of the century, by using the internal computer clock. Works for Windows can use such numbers to carry out mathematical operations using dates.

Formatting Field Cells:

As with a spreadsheet, each field can be given a specific number, or date/time format. A format set in any field of a database record, will force that format for the whole of that database field.

In our example, the date number can be converted to the current date by changing the format of the cell. With the date field selected, choose the **Format, Number** command, select **Date**, select the full date option (20 November 1994 in our case) and press **OK** to produce the date in the format shown. There are many different ways to show dates, as well as several 12- and 24- hour time formats. We will leave it to you to explore these other options. If the cell fills with the hash character (#), do not panic, it only means the date is too long for the cell width. Simply alter the cell width with the **Format, Field Size** command, or re-size it with the pointer..

The 'Total:' field, on our form, also needs formatting. Select it and choose **Format, Number**, **Currency,** with 2 decimal places, to show a leading '£' sign. Again adjust the cell width, if necessary.

Locking Fields:

All fields in a Works database are initially locked when first created. These locks, however, only become effective when they are 'activated', within the **Format, Protection** command. Not only do these locks prevent the data in a cell from being accidentally altered, but they also cause the <Tab> key to ignore the cell, when you are moving around the form, or entering data.

In our case, we need the current date cell to be protected, so we must unlock the other fields, before turning the protection facility on. Select each field in turn, and choose the command **Format, Protection** and cancel the **Data Locked** option. When all the fields, except 'Date:', have been unlocked, choose the **Format, Protection, Protect Data** command. The date field should now be fully protected. In fact, it is now inaccessible until database protection is toggled off again.

When you are completely happy with the design of a form you can lock the whole form, by selecting **Protect Form** in the Protection box.

Now complete the data entry by typing in the remaining 14 records shown in the screen dump on page 109. When you have saved the database as INVOICE1, a List view should then be the same as that printout.

Sorting a Database:

The records in our database are in the order in which they were entered, with the invoice numbers, in the 'Inv.No:' field, shown in ascending order. However, once records have been entered, you might find it easier to browse through the database if it were sorted in a different way; say, in alphabetical order of 'Customer Name:'. This might also make it easier to use the database for other operations, such as a mail merge. Works for Windows has an easy to use sort function, which can be accessed from either the Form or List screen.

With the cursor in any location, choose the **Tools**, **Sort Records** command. In the **1st Field** box, type the name of the first field to be sorted, in our case **Customer Name**, and select **Ascend A**. This sorts the field in an ascending order, from A - Z, and from 0 - 9. A descending sort order is the reverse. If you decide to have a secondary sort field (say you want invoices for the same company to appear in ascending order of invoice number), it is a simple matter to define a secondary sort range, before sorting. The three sort ranges available should be enough for most purposes.

Issuing these commands should produce the display shown on the next page.

Now re-sort the database, in ascending order on the 'Inv.No:' field, to return it to the original format.

Date Arithmetic:

There are several date functions which can be used in Works for Windows to carry out date calculations. For example, typing the function =DATE(89,4,18) - 18/4/89 backwards - works out the number of days since 31 December 1899. These functions are included to make Works more compatible with Lotus 1-2-3, but Works has an easier, and quicker, way of dealing with date arithmetic. Just typing a date into a cell, in one of the accepted date formats, allows Works for Windows to use the date number in any

File Edit View Insert Format Tools Window Help

Times New Roman   10

"AVON Construction

	Customer Name	Details	Inv.No	Issued	Paid	O/D	Total	
1	AVON Construction	Adhesive Tests	8902	11/08/94	1		£103.52	
2	BARROWS Associates	Tunnel Design Tests	8903	13/08/94	0		£99.32	
3	EALING Engines Dgn	Vibration Tests	8910	02/09/94	0		£58.95	
4	EUROBASE Co. Ltd	Proj. Contr. Manag.	8912	18/09/94	0		£150.00	
5	FREEMARKET Dealers	Stock Control Pack	8913	25/09/94	0		£560.00	
6	GLOWORM Ltd	Luminescence Tests	8907	20/08/94	0		£111.55	
7	HIRE Service Equip	Network Implement/n	8911	10/09/94	0		£290.00	
8	OILRIG Construct.	Metal Fatigue Tests	8914	03/10/94	0		£96.63	
9	PARKWAY Gravel	Material Size Tests	8905	20/08/94	0		£180.22	
10	SILVERSMITH Co	X-Ray Diffract. Test	8908	20/08/94	1		£123.45	
11	STONEAGE Ltd	Carbon Dating Tests	8904	15/08/94	0		£55.98	
12	TIME & Motion Ltd	Systems Analysis	8915	13/10/94	0		£120.35	
13	VORTEX Co. Ltd	Wind Tunnel Tests	8901	04/08/94	0		£120.84	
14	WESTWOOD Ltd	Load Bearing Tests	8906	20/08/94	0		£68.52	
15	WORMGLAZE Ltd	Heat Transfer Tests	8909	29/08/94	0		£35.87	
16								
17								
18								
19								

Press ALT to choose commands, or F2 to edit.   1   15/15

calculations. When a date is typed in a field, or a spreadsheet cell, what actually shows in that cell depends on the cell format. If '30/10/66', (a date in short date format), is typed into a cell, it will be shown as 30 October 1966 in long date format, or 24410, in any of the number formats.

The function

```
=NOW()-30/10/66
```

gives the difference in days (if the appropriate cell is formatted for integer numbers) between now and the mentioned date.

We will use this function to work out the number of overdue days for the unpaid invoices in our example, by typing the following formula into the O/D field cell:

```
=NOW()-Issued
```

However, before we proceed, we should take into consideration the fact that, normally, such information would not be necessary if an invoice has already been paid. Therefore, we need to edit the formula to make the result conditional on non-payment of the issued invoice.

The IF Function:

The =IF function allows comparison between two values with the use of special 'logical' operators. The logical operators we can use are listed below.

Logical operators

=	Equal to
<	Less than
>	Greater than
<=	Less than or Equal to
>=	Greater than or Equal to
<>	Not Equal to

The general format of the IF function is as follows:

=IF(Comparison, Outcome-if-true, Outcome-if-false)

which contains three arguments separated by commas. The first argument is the logical comparison, the second is what should happen if the outcome of the logical comparison is 'true', while the third is what should happen if the outcome of the logical comparison is 'false'.

Thus, we can incorporate an =IF function in the formula we entered in the O/D cell, to calculate the days overdue, only if the invoice has not been paid, otherwise '0' should be written into that cell. The test will be on the contents of the corresponding 'Paid' field of a record, and will look for anything else but '0'.

To edit the formula in the O/D cell, highlight the cell and press the Edit key (**F2**). Then press the <Home> cursor key, followed by →, to place the cursor after the '=' of the existing formula in the formula line at the top of the screen and insert

```
IF(Paid=0,
```

then press the <End> cursor key to move the cursor to the end of the existing entry and add

```
,0)
```

The edited formula should now correspond to that shown in the screen printout below.

	Customer Name	Details	Inv.No	Issued	Paid	O/D	Total	
1	VORTEX Co. Ltd	Wind Tunnel Tests	8901	04/08/94	0	109	£120.84	
2	AVON Construction	Adhesive Tests	8902	11/08/94	1	0	£103.52	
3	BARROWS Associates	Tunnel Design Tests	8903	13/08/94	0	100	£99.32	
4	STONEAGE Ltd	Carbon Dating Tests	8904	15/08/94	0	98	£55.98	
5	PARKWAY Gravel	Material Size Tests	8905	20/08/94	0	93	£180.22	
6	WESTWOOD Ltd	Load Bearing Tests	8906	20/08/94	0	93	£68.52	
7	GLOWORM Ltd	Luminescence Tests	8907	20/08/94	0	93	£111.55	
8	SILVERSMITH Co	X-Ray Diffract. Test	8908	20/08/94	1	0	£123.45	
9	WORMGLAZE Ltd	Heat Transfer Tests	8909	29/08/94	0	84	£35.87	
10	EALING Engines Dgn	Vibration Tests	8910	02/09/94	0	80	£58.95	
11	HIRE Service Equip	Network Implement/n	8911	10/09/94	0	72	£290.00	
12	EUROBASE Co. Ltd	Proj. Contr. Manag.	8912	18/09/94	0	64	£150.00	
13	FREEMARKET Dealers	Stock Control Pack.	8913	25/09/94	0	57	£560.00	
14	OILRIG Construct.	Metal Fatigue Tests	8914	03/10/94	0	49	£96.63	
15	TIME & Motion Ltd	Systems Analysis	8915	13/10/94	0	39	£120.35	
16								
17								
18								
19								

Note that once a formula is entered into any one field cell it is automatically copied to all the other cells in that field of the database. Save the file under the name INVOICE2.

Your results will almost certainly differ from those above. The reason for this is, of course, that the NOW() function returns different numerical values when used on different dates. To get the same results as those shown, you could reset your computer clock to that used in our example. This is easily done from the Windows Control Panel.

Save your work and Exit the Works for Windows program. Open the Control Panel (see Chapter 1, if necessary), double-click the Date/Time icon, reset the **Date** to '20/11/94' and press **OK**. Close the Control Panel and the new date will be operational when you re-enter Works for Windows.

WARNING - Make sure you have saved your work before doing this, and when you have finished this section remember to reset the date.

Searching a Database

A database can be searched for specific records, that meet several complex criteria, with the **View, Query** command, once a query has been set up with the **Tools, Create New Query** command. Or, more simply, by clicking the Toolbar Query View icon, shown here. For a simple search, on one field only, the **Edit, Find** command is, however, both quicker and easier.

We will use the previously saved database INVOICE2 to illustrate both these methods.

Let us assume we needed to find a record, from our database, containing the text 'x-ray'. In the form window, with any record showing, choose **Edit, Find**, type **x-ray** in the **Find What** box, and select the option, **All Records**. The record for 'SILVERSMITH Co' is brought to the screen, and the status line (1/15) indicates that this is the only record that meets the search criterion. To check this, press **F9** to switch to the List screen. Only the one record is shown, and all the others are hidden. The command, **View, Switch Hidden Records** will retrieve all the records which did not contain the searched for text (note that row 8 is not included in the listing). The **View, Show All Records** command will display the complete database again.

The same search sequence can be carried out in either the Form, or List, windows. In the Form window the whole database is always searched, whereas with List, if a part of the database has been selected, only that part will be searched. Otherwise the whole database is searched, as before.

Database Query:

Sometimes it is necessary to find records in a database that satisfy a variety of conditions. For example, in a warehouse stock database, you may need to find all the items that were purchased between May and July of last year, that were ordered by a specific person, cost between £5.00 and £100.00, and that remained in stock for more than 60 days. In Works for Windows this kind of search is called a query.

When a query is carried out in Works, all the records that match the query criteria are extracted. In List view these are all displayed, whereas in Form view you see one matching record at a time. Every time a query is applied the program searches the complete database for matches.

Retrieve the file INVOICE2.DBW, if it is not already loaded, and select the List view. Clicking the Query View icon presents a New Query box, as shown.

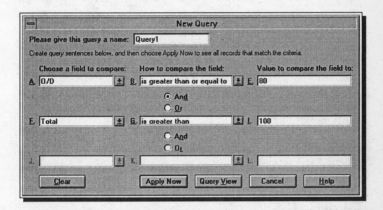

The above is completed assuming that we would like to search the database for all the details of our customers whose invoices are overdue by 80 or more days, and who owe more than £100.

This intuitive approach to queries is very much easier than having to develop long logical expressions yourself. In fact what is actually created, in the above case, is the expression

```
='O/D'>=VALUE("80")#AND#Total>VALUE("100")
```

which is placed in the 'O/D:' field cell of the query.

When all the required criteria have been entered, select the **Apply Now** button to action the query. Unless you have renamed it, this first query in your database will be Query1.

You are then returned to List view, where only the records which meet the search requirements will be listed. In our case this should be three only. The screen should now look similar to that shown next.

	Customer Name	Details	Inv.No	Issued	Paid	O/D	Total	
1	VORTEX Co. Ltd	Wind Tunnel Tests	8901	04/08/94	0	109	£120.84	
5	PARKWAY Gravel	Material Size Tests	8905	20/08/94	0	93	£180.22	
7	GLOWORM Ltd	Luminescence Tests	8907	20/08/94	0	93	£111.55	
16								
17								

To view all the records again, choose **View**, **Show All Records**. The query criteria will remain intact until next edited. To rapidly carry out a search, using existing criteria, simply press **F3**, which is a Quick Key for the **View**, **Apply Query** command, select the query and press <Enter>.

When you have several queries in a database you should give them each a sensible name, so that their functions are easy to remember. Now save this worksheet under the filename INVOICE3.

The Database Toolbar

As with the other tools, mouse users of Works for Windows have an advantage when using the database, in that they can make use of the Toolbar. Most of the icons are common to other Toolbars already described, but there are six icons on this bar specific to the database tool, whose meanings are as follows:

Option	*Result*
	Change to Form view
	Change to List view
	Change to Query view
	Change to Report view
	Insert field
	Insert new record

8. DATABASE APPLICATIONS

Once a database has been created, the data sorted in the required order, and specific records have been searched for, the retrieved data can be browsed on the screen, either one record at a time, or in the list format, one full screen at a time. Some form of hard copy will almost certainly be required at some stage, by printing part, or all, of the database to paper.

Printing from a Database

There are three main ways of printing information from a database. In the 'Form' view, selected records are printed out in the same format as the screen form. Printing from a 'List' view will produce rows and columns just as they appear on the screen; little manipulation of the printed result is possible. To obtain a customised print-out, possibly containing selected fields only, but with report and page titles, totals and sub-totals, a 'Report' must first be defined. Data can then be printed from the Report screen.

What is printed from the List and Form windows is controlled by the settings in the **File**, **Page Setup**, **Other Options** dialogue box, as shown overleaf. Printing from List view, will produce a spreadsheet like layout, which will only be of use, if your database has only a few fields per record.

Printing from the Form view could probably be best used with a diary type appointment database, or with a simple database designed to hold, say, personnel lists or parts inventories. Space could maybe be built into each form to hold a scanned photograph for example.

To demonstrate the process, load the database INVOICE3.WDB, which was created in the last chapter. From the Form view choose **File**, **Page Setup**, **Other Options** to display the dialogue box shown overleaf.

Switch off **Page breaks between records**, type '1' as the **Space between records**, and select **All items** as in our example. When you accept these settings a print preview should show three neatly spaced records on the page.

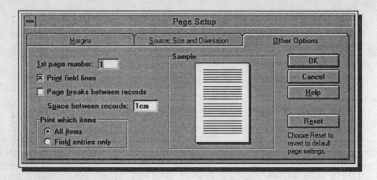

Creating a Report

A report can present records sorted and grouped, with summaries, totals, and with explanatory text. Once a report format has been set up, producing a report is a quick, almost automatic process. The current records 'displayed' in a database are those used to make the body of a report. The initial process is to create a report definition, which indicates what information will be in a report, and where it will be placed. Microsoft have given the Report facility of Works for Windows a 'semi-automatic front end' and the production of simple report formats is now very much easier.

Using the database we built up in the last chapter, we will step through the process of setting up a report definition. If necessary, retrieve the file saved as INVOICE3.WDB. This was a database to store details of the invoices sent out by a small company. It would be very useful, for both the accountant and the company management, if a report like that on the next page could be 'instantly' produced, and printed out. This summarises all the unpaid invoices and ranks them in groups depending on the number of months they have been overdue. Once we have defined the format of this report, it will only take a few keystrokes, at any time in the future, to produce a similar but updated report.

Change to the Form screen of INVOICE3.WDB, as we must first add an extra field to the form. This will show the number of months an invoice is overdue. We will need it, to provide the basis for sorting the database records, and breaking them up into groups.

ADEPT CONSULTANTS LTD
Invoice Analysis Report

Summary of Overdue Invoices

Customer Name	Invoice Number	Days Overdue	Total Amount
TIME & Motion Ltd	8915	39	£120.35
OILRIG Construct.	8914	49	£96.63
FREEMARKET Dealers	8913	57	£560.00
1 - 2 Months Overdue	3	48	£776.98
EUROBASE Co. Ltd	8912	64	£150.00
HIRE Service Equip	8911	72	£290.00
EALING Engines Dgn	8910	80	£58.95
WORMGLAZE Ltd	8909	84	£35.87
2 - 3 Months Overdue	4	75	£534.82
PARKWAY Gravel	8905	93	£180.22
WESTWOOD Ltd	8906	93	£68.52
GLOWORM Ltd	8907	93	£111.55
STONEAGE Ltd	8904	98	£55.98
BARROWS Associates	8903	100	£99.32
VORTEX Co. Ltd	8901	109	£120.84
3 - 4 Months Overdue	6	98	£636.43
Overall Totals and Averages	13	79	£1,948.23

Insert a new field called 'Months:', placed wherever you like on the form, but give it a width of 3. Highlight the empty cell, type the formula

=Int(O/D/30)

and press <Enter>. Note that Works for Windows places single inverted commas around the field name O/D, to show it as a label; this is because it contains the slash character '/'. The formula produces the integer part of the number of days overdue, divided by thirty. In other words, the whole number of months overdue.

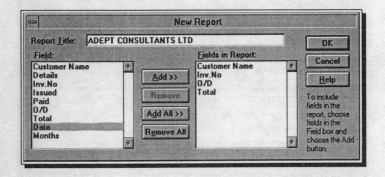

We are now ready to create the report definition. Choose the **Tools**, **Create New Report** command, or click the Toolbar Report View icon shown here. The New Report dialogue box is opened.

To complete the box as shown, type ADEPT CONSULTANTS LTD into the **Report Title** box. Select the field 'Customer Name' in the **Field** list box and press **Add>>**, or <Alt+A>, to add the field to the **Fields in Report** list. In the same way add the fields 'Inv.No', 'O/D' and 'Total' and then choose **OK** to select the dialogue box options.

The Report Statistics box is then shown. This provides a quick way of entering formulae into the report, to carry out calculations and produce totals or averages, for example. In the future you should find this an easy way to generate rapid reports, but at this stage we will not use this method, so press **OK** to move to the report definition screen, shown on the next page.

The message in the pop-up box tells you to use the Print Preview to see what your report will look like when printed.

The working area of the screen contains columns and rows which intersect, as in the spreadsheet, to form cells.

The row types, shown on the left part of the screen, determine the order the rows will be printed in the report, and what action will be taken in that row.

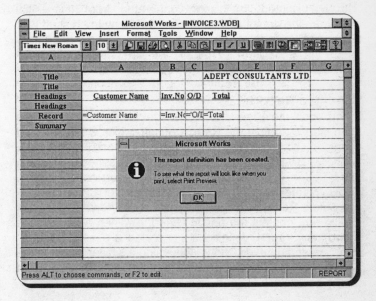

Row type	Prints
Title	At the beginning of a report
Headings	At the top of each page
Intr *1st breakfield*	At the beginning of each group created by the 1st breakfield
Intr *2nd breakfield*	At the beginning of each group created by the 2nd breakfield
Intr *3rd breakfield*	At the beginning of each group created by the 3rd breakfield
Record	Each displayed record
Summ *3rd breakfield*	At the end of each group created by the 3rd breakfield
Summ *2nd breakfield*	At the end of each group created by the 2nd breakfield
Summ *1st breakfield*	At the end of each group created by the 1st breakfield
Summary	At the end of a report

At this stage the 'Intr' and 'Summ' line types do not appear on our screen, as there are no breakpoints defined for the report.

If you printed the report generated from this initial procedure we don't think you would be overly impressed with the results. As long as you can persevere, though, and follow us to the end of the chapter, we are sure you will be impressed with the power of the report generating facility.

Naming a Report:

If you open the **View** sub-menu you will see that a '√' has been placed against the **Report** option, which when selected opens a box showing the option **Report1.** Works for Windows gives any reports generated a series of names, numbered 1, 2, 3, etc. To change this report name, choose **Tools**, **Name Report**, type 'Overdue' in the **Name** text box and select **Rename** followed by **OK**. The **View**, **Report** box should now contain the option Overdue. When a database is saved, any report definitions generated are saved with it, including sorting instructions. Obtaining a similar report in the future is simply a matter of selecting it from the **View**, **Report** box.

Defining a Report:

The definition to automatically produce the report on page 125 is shown in the next screen dump example. This was designed to print on an A4 sheet of paper.

As an example we will step through the procedure of producing this report. Most of the reporting features should become apparent during the operation. You may also find it useful to spend a few minutes with the relevant section of the Works for Windows tutorial.

The report definition will be easier to prepare from an empty work area, so choose **Edit**, **Select All** and then **Edit, Clear** to clear the working area cells.

The first operation is to reset the column widths. Set columns A, B and C to a width of 2, by selecting these columns, choosing **Format, Column Width** and typing 2, followed by <Enter>. In the same way, alter the other columns as follows: D, E and F to 17and G to 16.

File   Edit   View   Tools   Window   Help

Times New Roman   10

	A	B	C	D	E	F	G
				=Customer Name			
Title				ADEPT CONSULTANTS LTD			
Title				Invoice Analysis Report			
Title							
Title				Summary of Overdue Invoices			
Title							
Title							
Headings	Customer				Invoice	Days	Total
Headings	Name				Number	Overdue	Amount
Headings							
Headings							
Record				=Inv.No	='O/D'	=Total	
Summ Months							
Summ Months							
Summ Months	=I-	=(Months Overdue		=COUNT('O/D')	=AVG('O/D')	=SUM(Total)	
Summ Months							
Summ Months							
Summary	Overall Totals						
Summary	and Averages			=COUNT('O/D')	=AVG('O/D')	=SUM(Total)	
Summary							

Press ALT to choose commands, or F2 to edit.   REPORT

Adding a Report Title:

The 'Title' rows hold any text that is to appear at the top of the first printed page of the report. In our example we will need six rows of this type, so we must insert four more. Press <Ctrl+Home> to move the cursor to the Home cell, highlight the top two cells of row A by pressing, **F8** followed by the down arrow, choose **Insert**, **Row/Column** and select **Row** in the dialogue box. The next box asks what type of rows are to be inserted; we want 'Title', which is highlighted, so press <Enter> to complete the operation. As we highlighted two rows initially, two new ones should have been inserted. Repeat the operation to insert a further two rows, making six in all.

To position the main report title in the centre of the printed page, move the cursor to column A of the top row, type

```
ADEPT   CONSULTANTS   LTD
```

and press <Enter>. We will leave it to you to add the other two title lines in column A of rows 2 and 4. Now highlight the first four rows of columns A to G and use the **Format**, **Alignment**, **Center across selection** command.

129

To place the horizontal line across the page, select the cells A5 to G5 and place a **Bottom** line with the **Format**, **Border** command. There are several line options to choose from.

Adding Page Titles:

Page titles are placed in 'Headings' type rows, and appear below the report title on the first page of a report, and at the top of all subsequent pages. We will need four of these type of rows, so insert two more, as described earlier. The top two of these rows will hold the four report column titles, as shown on page 125. To enter these, place:

Customer and Name	-	left aligned	-	in column A
Invoice and Number	-	centre aligned	-	in column E
Days and Overdue	-	centre aligned	-	in column F
Total and Amount	-	right aligned	-	in column G

The way to select the above alignments is from the **Format**, **Alignment** box. Produce any lines with the **Format**, **Border** command, as described previously.

Using Formulae in a Cell:

The body of the report will be produced by the contents of the 'Record' row. If we type a field name, preceded by an equals sign, in a 'Record' cell, Works places the contents of that field for each record into the report.

There are also a series of statistical operators that can be included in cell formulae. These are mainly used in 'Summ' type rows, to produce totals, averages, etc. When placed in a 'Summ fieldname' row they give field statistics for the previous group printed. In a 'Summary' row the statistics refer to that field for the whole report.

Statistic	*Calculates*
SUM	Total of the group
AVG	Average of the group
COUNT	Number of items in the group
MAX	Largest number in the group
MIN	Smallest number in the group
STD	Standard deviation of the group
VAR	Variance of the group

There are several ways to enter formulae in a cell. If you can remember all your database fields, you could simply type the formulae in.

Insert, **Field Name** places the selected field name in a cell, **Insert**, **Field Entry** places an '=' followed by the name; both dialogue boxes list all the fields of the database. The **Insert**, **Field Summary** box lists not only the database fields, but all the above functions, which you can select to place formulae in a 'Summ', or 'Summary', type row.

In our example, to complete the 'Record' row, enter the following formulae into the cells shown below and format the cells, in the **Format**, **Number** box as follows:

Cell	Contents	Alignment	Format
A	=Customer Name	Left justified	
E	=Inv.No.	Centre justified	Fixed (0)
F	=O/D	Centre justified	Fixed (0)
G	=Total	Right justified	Currency (2)

Sorting a Report:

A report is sorted to arrange the database entries in a certain order, such as alphabetical (order) or by date. A sort order specified in a report stays with that report, until it is physically changed. The main sort field, in our case, is on the Months field. We must specify the sort parameters now, as 'Summ' type rows cannot be used without a breakpoint having been entered.

The **Tools**, **Sort Records** command will produce a dialogue box similar to the one below. The selections shown are those required for our example. To obtain them, type 'Months' in the **1st Field**, select an **Ascend A** search and force a break, <Alt+G>, on this field.

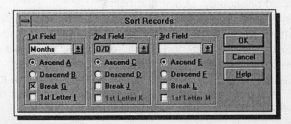

This will cause the report to split its output every time the value of the field 'Months' changes. In our case, for neatness, we have also specified a **2nd Field** ascending sort on the 'O/D' field. If our database contained many hundreds of records, with several for each customer, we could also sort; and break, on the 'Customer Name' field. A summary for each customer would then be produced.

When the Sort Records dialogue box is accepted, an extra row, 'Summ Months', is placed in the report definition. Note that a series of simple formulae is also inserted in this new line. In our case, most of these are not a lot of use, as can be demonstrated by looking at the report so far produced.

From the definition screen this can be done by clicking on the Print Preview Toolbar icon, and pressing **Cancel** will return you to the previous screen. Clear the formulae in columns A to G, with the **Edit, Clear** command.

Completing the Report Definition:

Insert four more 'Summ Months' rows, and enter the following formulae in the middle row cells, with the formats and styles shown, as before.

Cell	Contents	Alignment	Format
A	=Months	Left justified	Fixed (0)
B	"–	Left justified	
C	=Months+1	Right justified	Fixed (0)
D	" Months Overdue	Left justified	
E	=COUNT('O/D')	Centre justified	Fixed (0)
F	=AVG('O/D')	Centre justified	Fixed (0)
G	=SUM(Total)	Left justified	Currency (2)

When you have completed this row, place horizontal lines, as described previously, above and below it.

Our report definition is almost complete now, only the 'Summary' rows remain to be done. If you have worked your way to this stage, entering these rows on your own should present no problems.

Insert two more 'Summary' type rows. Place a line in the bottom one, and type the following in the remaining two rows:

Cell	Contents	Alignment	Format
Row 17			
A	"Overall Totals	Left justified	
Row 18			
A	"and Averages	Left justified	
E	=COUNT(O/D)	Centre justified	Fixed (0)
F	=AVG(O/D)	Centre justified	Fixed (0)
G	=SUM(Total)	Right justified	Currency (2)

Applying a Query:

For a report to show the correct records, the database must first be searched using the required retrieval criteria, as was described in the previous chapter.

In our case, the report should include all the invoices which have not been settled. Choose **Tools**, **Create New Query**, select the field 'Paid' in **A**, select the statement 'is equal to' in **B** and type '0' in **E**. Press **Apply Now** and the correct records should now be active. You could use the List View icon to check that the Query has worked.

Printing a Report:

Printing a report is similar to printing a word processor document, except that the facility to force column page breaks is included, as is the case with spreadsheets. From the Report screen choose **File**, **Page Setup** and make sure your page is set up with a 1.5" left margin, and select Print Preview to see what your report will look like on paper. It should be similar to the screen dump shown on the next page. Press **P** to start printing, or **Cancel** to return to the Report definition screen.

Our report definition is now complete. It probably took several hours to build, but an instant report can now be generated from it, no matter how big the database gets. Also you should by now be able to tackle any reports of your own design.

ADEPT CONSULTANTS LTD
Invoice Analysis Report

Summary of Overdue Invoices

Customer Name	Invoice Number	Days Overdue	Total Amount
TIME & Motion Ltd	8915	39	£120.35
OIL RIG Construct.	8914	49	£96.63
FREEMARKET Dealers	8913	57	£560.00
1 - 2 Months Overdue	3	48	£776.98
EUROBASE Co Ltd	8912	64	£150.00
HIRE Service Equip	8911	72	£290.00
EALING Engines Dan	8910	80	£58.95
WORMGLAZE Ltd	8909	84	£35.87
2 - 3 Months Overdue	4	75	£534.82
PARKWAY Gravel	8905	93	£180.22
WESTWOOD Ltd	8906	93	£68.52
GLOW CIRM Ltd	8907	93	£111.55
STONEAGE Ltd	8904	98	£55.98
BARROWS Associates	8903	100	£99.32
VORTEX Co. Ltd	8901	109	£120.84
3 - 4 Months Overdue	6	98	£636.43
Overall Totals and Averages	13	79	£1,948.23

Page 1

Previous

Next

Zoom In

Zoom Out

Print

Cancel

Form Letters

We are now in a position to use the mail merge capability of Works for Windows to create customised 'form letters', which make use of information stored in a database. As an example of this, you could create the simple database shown next, which contains the personal details of our potential customers. Save it as ADDRESS.WDB.

Now type the letter shown below it, using the word processor. Note the way the various field names are enclosed by angled brackets. These 'field name markers' cannot be just typed in place. Move the cursor to where you want a field name marker and choose the **Insert**, **Database Field** command. Click the **Database** button and select the file name of the database to use, in our case ADDRESS.WDB. In the **Fields** box select the field name you want press **insert** and then **Close** the box. Works will place the field name in the document. When the letter is completed save the document as LETTER.WPS.

Note the field 'Appellation' which could be 'Sir', if you didn't know the name of the recipient, 'Mr Brown', if you did or 'John', if he was a friend of yours.

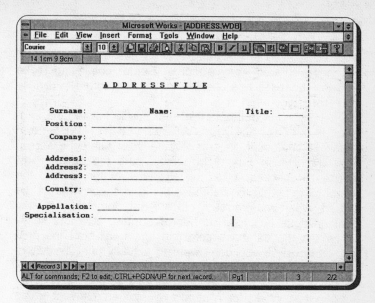

The field 'Specialisation' is included so that your form letters are only sent to relevant people. You would use information in this field in a Query to select records.

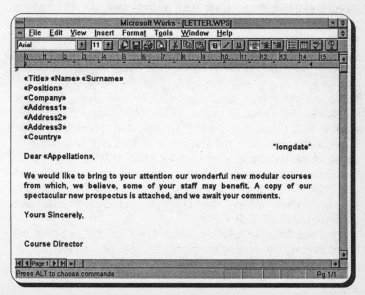

Printing Form Letters:

Works for Windows will print one copy of the letter for each record displayed in the database, assuming of course that you have entered some records. Before continuing make sure the database has been searched and sorted to display the records you need.

Open both the database file and the file holding the form letter. In our case ADDRESS.WDB and LETTER.WPS. From the word processor file, make sure your printer is set up correctly, choose **File**, **Print**, make sure the option **Print Merge** is checked, click the **Preview** button, select the database to use in the database box and check what will be printed. When you are ready select **Print**, complete the usual Print dialogue box for **Number of copies**, etc., and finally confirming the database selection again will start the print run. Obviously if you don't want to actually print the letters you would press **Cancel**.

That is all there is to it. As long as your printer does not run out of paper, Works for Windows will print as many letters as there are records selected.

This procedure is not, of course, restricted to producing letters. It can be used for any word processed document which extracts information from a database.

9. OTHER PROGRAM FEATURES

The Communications Tool

Works for Windows 3.0 includes a Communications tool that helps you to connect your computer to other distant ones and to exchange information between them. This usually entails transferring information over a telephone line, with a modem. You can also directly connect your computer to another with a special cable.

We do not have space in this book to cover this aspect of Works, so a very brief overview only is included. The basic steps in communications are:

- Creating a Communications file
- Adjusting settings
- Connecting
- Exchanging information
- Disconnecting

After your first session with another computer, you can save all your settings with the Communications file. The name of the computer will then appear at the bottom of the Phone menu. The next time you want to connect to that same computer, just choose it from the Phone menu, and Works will make the connection for you.

For more information about this tool, we suggest you work through the tutorial lesson 'Introducing Communications'; and then use the **Help**, **Contents** command, click on the *Communications* icon and page through the many Help screens with the <u><<</u> and <u>>></u> buttons.

There are two more features included in the Works for Windows package that need some coverage. These are WorksWizards and Templates, both of which are designed to make the program more useful and easier to use.

WorksWizards

With WorksWizards, new to the Windows version of Microsoft Works, you get step-by-step assistance in creating particular types of applications. There are 12 WorksWizards with Version 3.0, set up for creating such applications as; an address book database, personalised form letters, mailing labels and many more. WorksWizards are produced by Microsoft and cannot be 'home made'; presumably they will continue to offer additions to the range in the future.

To start a WorksWizard use the **File**, **WorksWizards** command, or click the **Use a WorksWizard** button from the Startup box. These both open a box offering you the following choice of WorksWizards.

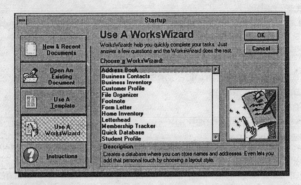

An Address Book is used by most people so it would make sense to select this database option first. Work your way through the initial screens, selecting from the extra field, and database style options offered, pressing the **Next** button to get to the next screen, whenever necessary.

When all the fields required have been chosen, press the **Create** button, when it is offered, and sit back for a few minutes.

WorksWizards goes into 'automatic mode' and with much flashing of screens builds up your database. In fact an in-built macro comes into operation, which is quite fun to watch.

The last screen, shown on the facing page, shows the Form view of your new very professionally produced database

You must agree that this is an easy way to create a new database, which even offers quite a degree of customisation along the way.

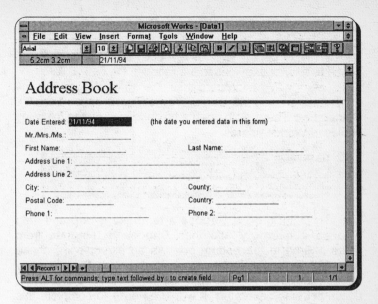

We strongly recommend you experiment with these automated procedures. They can often produce the results you want in a very short time. We have not spent much time explaining them, or covered them earlier in the book, for two very good reasons:

1. They are very user friendly and almost anyone should be able to work through them without too many problems.

2. We feel strongly that you will become more proficient with the Works for Windows program, as a whole, if you build your own applications.

Templates

A Template is a document 'blank' which can contain titles, text, formatting and other features, which do not change between documents of the same type. You can open a Template, rename it and then adapt it to whatever you need.

To access the Templates provided with Works 3.0 use the **File**, **Templates** menu command, or click on **Use a Template** in the Startup box. It would take many hours to work through the many Templates provided.

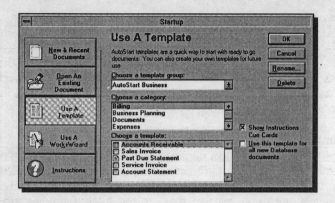

The first thing to do is **Choose a template group** and then **Choose a category** and then **Choose a template** from those offered in the bottom box. As an example we chose AutoStart Personal, Documents, Résumé, (or CV in slightly more traditional English). Another very professional document was generated. It would be easy to complete this and have your own well produced CV, which in today's job climate, might be very useful indeed.

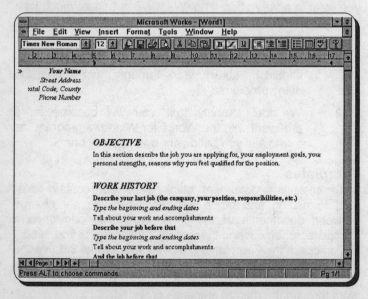

You can use any document as the basis for a Template. When you are happy with its layout and contents, choose the **File**, **Save As** command, select the **Template** button, type a **Template Name** and press **OK**. Whenever you want to use your new Template, choose the Custom Template group from the Use a Template box and you should see its name in the available Template list.

Sample Files:
The Works for Windows package should have installed some sample files on your hard disc during the Setup process. On our installation, four were placed in the **\msworks\samples** directory, and you will find more in the tutorial subdirectory **msworks.cbt**.

All of these files can be opened in the usual way with the **File**, **Open Existing File** command, the tutorial ones cannot be modified however. Some you might find to be very useful, and worth customising, or copying, for your own needs; whereas some are probably only worth deleting.

* * *

Works for Windows has more commands and functions which can be used to build and run your applications and to link with other applications in special ways. What this book has tried to do is to introduce you to the overall subject and give you a solid foundation on which to build your future knowledge.

* * *

APPENDIX A
FUNCTIONS

Microsoft Work's =functions are built-in formulae that perform specialised calculations in both spreadsheets and databases. Their general format is:

=name(arg1,arg2,...)

where 'name' is the function name, and 'arg1', 'arg2', etc., are the arguments required for the evaluation of the function. Arguments must appear in a parenthesised list as shown above and their exact number depends on the function being used. However, there are seven functions that do not require arguments and are used with empty parentheses. These are: =ERR( ), =FALSE( ), =NA( ), =NOW( ), =PI( ), =RAND( ) and =TRUE( ).

There are three types of arguments used with =functions: numeric values, range values and text strings, the type used being dependent on the type of function. Numeric value arguments can be entered either directly as numbers, as a cell address, a cell range name or as a formula. Range value arguments can be entered either as a range address or a range name.

In the spreadsheet tool you can now automatically choose a function with the **Insert**, **Function** command and Works inserts it, including its arguments, into the formula bar.

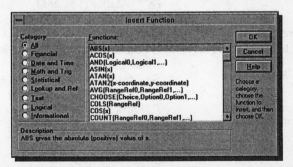

When used in a database, functions apply only to the fields in the same record of the database.

Types of Functions

There are several types of functions, such as mathematical, logical, financial, statistical, date and time, text, reference and informational. Each type requires their own number and type of arguments. These are listed below under the various function categories.

Mathematical Functions:

Mathematical functions evaluate a result using numeric arguments. The various functions and their meaning are as follows:

Function	Description
=ABS(X)	Returns the absolute value of X
=ACOS(X)	Returns the angle in radians, whose cosine is X (arc cos of X)
=ASIN(X)	Returns the angle in radians, whose sine is X (arc sin of X)
=ATAN(X)	Returns the angle (radians), between $\pi/2$ and $-\pi/2$, whose tangent is X (arc tan of X – 2 quadrant)
=ATAN2(X,Y)	Returns the angle (radians), between π and $-\pi$ whose tangent is Y/X (arc tan of Y/X – 4 quadrant)
=COS(X)	Returns the cosine of angle X, (X must be in radians)
=EXP(X)	Raises e to the power of X
=INT(X)	Returns the integer part of X
=LN(X)	Returns the natural logarithm (base e) of X
=LOG(X)	Returns the logarithm (base 10) of X
=MOD(X,Y)	Returns the remainder of X/Y
=PI( )	Returns the value of π (3.141593)
=RAND( )	Returns a random number between 0 and 1, excluding 1
=ROUND(X,N)	Returns the value of X rounded to N places

=SIN(X)	Returns the sine of angle X (X must be in radians)
=SQRT(X)	Returns the square root of X
=TAN(X)	Returns the tangent of angle X (X must be in radians).

Logical Functions:

Logical functions produce a value based on the result of a conditional statement, using numeric arguments. The various functions and their meanings are as follows:

Function	Description
=AND(Ag0,Ag1..)	Returns 1 (TRUE) if all of the arguments are true, else returns 0 (FALSE)
=FALSE( )	Returns the logical value 0
=IF(Cr,X,Y)	Returns the value X if Cr is TRUE and Y if Cr is FALSE
=OR(Ag0,Ag1..)	Returns 1 (TRUE) if any of the arguments are true, else returns 0 (FALSE)
=TRUE( )	Returns the logical value 1.

Financial Functions:

Financial functions evaluate loans, annuities, and cash flows over a period of time, using numeric arguments. The various functions and their meaning are as follows:

Function	Description
=CTERM(Rt,Fv,Pv)	Returns the number of compounding periods for an investment of present value Pv, to grow to a future value Fv, at a fixed interest rate Rt
=DDB(Ct,Sg,Lf,Pd)	Returns the double-declining depreciation allowance of an asset, given the original cost Ct, predicted salvage value Sg, the life Lf of the asset, and the period Pd

=FV(Pt,Rt,Tm)	Returns the future value of a series of equal payments, each of equal amount Pt, earning a periodic interest rate Rt, over a number of payment periods in term Tm
=IRR(Gs,Rg)	Returns the internal rate of return of the series of cash flows in a range Rg, based on the approximate percentage guess Gs of the IRR
=NPV(Rt,Rg)	Returns the present value of the series of future cash flows in range Rg, discounted at a periodic interest rate Rt
=PMT(Pl,Rt,Tm)	Returns the amount of the periodic payment needed to pay off the principal Pl, at a periodic interest rate Rt, over the number of payment periods in term Tm
=PV(Pt,Rt,Tm)	Returns the present value of a series of equal payments, each of equal amount Pt, discounted at a periodic interest rate Rt, over a number of payment periods in term Tm
=RATE(Fv,Pv,Tm)	Returns the periodic interest rate necessary for a present value Pv to grow to a future value Fv, over the number of compounding periods in term Tm
=SLN(Ct,Sg,Lf)	Returns the straight-line depreciation allowance of an asset for one period, given the original cost Ct, predicted salvage value Sg, and the life Lf of the asset
=SYD(Ct,Sg,Lf,Pd)	Returns the sum-of-the-years' digits depreciation allowance of an asset, given the original cost

Ct, predicted salvage value Sg, the life Lf of the asset, and the period Pd

=TERM(Pt,Rt,Fv) Returns the number of payment periods of an investment, given the amount of each payment Pt, the periodic interest rate Rt, and the future value of the investment Fv.

Statistical Functions:

Statistical functions evaluate lists of values using numeric arguments or cell ranges. The various functions and their meaning are as follows:

Function	Description
=AVG(Rg0,Rg1,..)	Returns the average of values in range(s) Rg0, Rg1,...
=COUNT(Rg0,Rg1,..)	Returns the number of non-blank entries in range(s) Rg0, Rg1,..
=MAX(Rg0,Rg1,..)	Returns the maximum value in range(s) Rg0, Rg1,..
=MIN(Rg0,Rg1,..)	Returns the minimum value in range(s) Rg0, Rg1,..
=STD(Rg0,Rg1,..)	Returns the standard deviation of values in range(s) Rg0, Rg1,..
=SUM(Rg0,Rg1,..)	Returns the sum of values in range(s) Rg0, Rg1,..
=VAR(Rg0,Rg1,..)	Returns the variance of values in range(s) Rg0, Rg1,..

Text Functions:

Text functions operate on strings and produce numeric or string values dependent on the function.

Function	Description
=EXACT(Sg1,Sg2)	Returns 1 (TRUE) if strings Sg1 and Sg2 are exactly alike, otherwise 0 (FALSE)

=FIND(Ss,Sg,Sn)	Returns position at which the first occurrence of search string Ss begins in string Sg, starting the search from search number Sn
=LEFT(Sg,N)	Returns the first (leftmost) N characters in string Sg
=LENGTH(Sg)	Returns the number of characters in string Sg
=LOWER(Sg)	Converts all the letters in string Sg to lowercase
=MID(Sg,Sn,N)	Returns N characters from string Sg beginning with the character at Sn
=N(Rg)	Returns the numeric value in the upper left corner cell in range Rg
=PROPER(Sg)	Converts all words in string Sg to first letter in uppercase and the rest in lowercase
=REPEAT(Sg,N)	Returns string Sg N times. Unlike the repeating character (\), the output is not limited by the column width
=REPLACE(O,S,N,Ns)	Removes N characters from original string O, starting at character S and then inserts new string Ns in the vacated place
=RIGHT(Sg,N)	Returns the last (rightmost) N characters in string Sg
=S(Rg)	Returns the string value in the upper left corner cell in range Rg
=STRING(X,N)	Returns the numeric value X as a string, with N decimal places
=TRIM(Sg)	Returns string Sg with no leading, trailing or consecutive spaces
=UPPER(Sg)	Converts all letters in string Sg to uppercase
=VALUE(Sg)	Returns the numeric value of string Sg.

Date and Time Functions:

Date and time functions generate and use serial numbers to represent dates and times. Each date between 1 January, 1900 and 31 December 2079 has an integer serial number starting with 1 and ending with 65534. Each moment during a day has a decimal serial number starting with 0.000 at midnight and ending with 0.99999 just before the following midnight. Thus the value 0.5 indicates midday. The various functions and their meanings are as follows:

Function	Description
=DATE(Yr,Mh,Dy)	Returns the date number of Yr,Mh,Dy
=DAY(Dn)	Returns the day number of date number Dn
=HOUR(Tn)	Returns the hour number of time number Tn
=MINUTE(Tn)	Returns the minute number of time number Tn
=MONTH(Dn)	Returns the month number of date number Dn
=NOW( )	Returns the serial number for the current date and time
=SECOND(Tn)	Returns the second number of time number Tn
=TIME(Hr,Ms,Ss)	Returns the time number of Hr,Ms,Ss
=YEAR(Dn)	Returns the year number of date number Dn.

Special Functions:

Special functions perform a variety of advanced tasks, such as looking up a value in a table. or providing other information. The various functions and their meaning are as follows:

Function	Description
=CHOOSE(X,V0,..,Vn)	Returns the Xth value in the list V0,..,Vn
=COLS(Rg)	Returns the number of columns in the range Rg

=ERR( )	Returns the value of ERR
=HLOOKUP(X,Rg,Rn)	Performs a horizontal table look-up by comparing the value X to each cell in the top row, or index row, in range Rg, then moves down the column in which a match is found by the specified row number Rn
=INDEX(Rg,Cn,Rw)	Returns the value of the cell in range at the intersection of column Cn and row Rw
=ISERR(X)	Returns 1 (TRUE) if X contains ERR, else returns 0 (FALSE)
=ISNA(X)	Returns 1 (TRUE) if X contains N/A, else returns 0 (FALSE)
=NA( )	Returns the numeric value of N/A
=ROWS(Rg)	Returns the number of rows in range Rg
=VLOOKUP(X,Rg,Cn)	Performs a vertical table look-up by comparing the value X to each cell in the first column, or index column, in range Rg, then moves across the row in which a match is found by the specified column number Cn.

APPENDIX B
QUICK KEY COMBINATIONS

Navigation Keys

Moving Between Windows:

To switch to	*Press*
Next pane	F6
Next document window	Ctrl+F6
Previous pane	Shift+F6
Previous document window	Ctrl+Shift+F6
Next application window	Alt+Tab
Previous application window	Shift+Alt+Esc
The Task List	Ctrl+Esc
Close the active document window	Ctrl+F4
Close the active application	Alt+F4

Moving in a Dialogue Box:

You can also choose a dialogue box option by pressing the Alt key and the underlined letter in the option name.

To	*Press*
Move forward through options	Tab
Move backward through options	Shift+Tab
Open a list box	↓
Confirm an option or carry it out	Enter
Cancel changes and close	Esc

Moving in a Document:

To move	*Press*
To a bookmark	F5
To next bookmark	Shift+F5
To the beginning of line	Home
To the end of line	End
To the beginning of document	Ctrl+Home
To the end of document	Ctrl+End
Down one line	↓
Up one line	↑
To the previous paragraph	Ctrl+↑ *(WP only)*
To the next paragraph	Ctrl+↓ *(WP only)*
Left one character	←

Right one character	→
To the previous word	Ctrl+←
To the next word	Ctrl+→
To the top of document window	Ctrl+PgUp
To the bottom of document window	Ctrl+PgDn

To scroll	*Press*
Up one window	PgUp
Down one window	PgDn

Moving in a Spreadsheet:

To move	*Press*
To particular cell, range or row	F5
To the next named range	Shift+F5
To the previous cell in range	Shift+Enter
To the next cell in a range	Enter
To the beginning of row	Home
To the end of row	End
To the beginning of spreadsheet	Ctrl+Home
To the end of spreadsheet	Ctrl+End
Up one cell	↑
Down one cell	↓
Left one cell	← or Shift+Tab
Right one cell	→ or Tab
Up to the first or last cell of a range	Ctrl+↑
Down to the first or last cell of a range	Ctrl+↓
Left to the first or last cell of a range	Ctrl+←
Right to the first or last cell of a range	Ctrl+→

To scroll	*Press*
Up one window	PgUp
Down one window	PgDn
Left one window	Ctrl+PgUp
Right one window	Ctrl+PgDn

Moving in a Database or Report:

To move	*Press*
Left through the database or report	←
Right through the database or report	→
To previous unlocked field	Shift+Tab
To next unlocked field	Tab
To the beginning of database	Ctrl+Home

To the end of database	Ctrl+End
Up one field	↑
Down one field	↓
Up to the top or previous record	Ctrl+↑
Down to the last or next record	Ctrl+↓

To move in list view	*Press*
To the beginning of a record	Home
To the end of record	End
Left to the first field	Ctrl+←
Right to the last field	Ctrl+→

To move in form view	*Press*
To the left margin of a form	Home
To the right margin of a form	End
To the previous record	Ctrl+PgUp
To the next record	Ctrl+PgDn
Up one window	PgUp
Down one window	PgDn

To scroll in list view	*Press*
Up one window	PgUp
Down one window	PgDn
Right one window	Ctrl+PgDn
Left one window	Ctrl+PgUp

To scroll in form view	*Press*
Horizontally one window to left	Ctrl+←
Horizontally one window to right	Ctrl+→

Highlighting Keys

Highlighting in the Word Processor:

To	*Press*
Extend a selection	F8
Quit extending	Esc
Collapse a selection	Shift+F8

To highlight	*Press*
A word	F8 twice
A sentence	F8 three times
A paragraph	F8 four times
A document	F8 five times
The previous character	Shift+←

The next character	Shift+→
The previous word	Ctrl+Shift+←
The next word	Ctrl+Shift+→
To the beginning of line	Shift+Home
To the end of line	Shift+End
To the beginning of document	Ctrl+Shift+Home
To the end of document	Ctrl+Shift+End
To the previous line	Shift+↑
To the next line	Shift+↓
To the previous paragraph	Ctrl+Shift+↑
To the next paragraph	Ctrl+Shift+↓
To the previous window	Shift+PgUp
To the next window	Shift+PgDn
To the top of the window	Ctrl+Shift+PgUp
To the bottom of the window	Ctrl+Shift+PgDn

Highlighting in the Spreadsheet:

A cell is highlighted by moving to that cell; a border around the cell shows it is highlighted.

To highlight	*Press*
A row	Ctrl+F8
A column	Shift+F8
An entire spreadsheet	Ctrl+Shift+F8
Left one cell	Shift+←
Left to the first or last cell of a range	Ctrl+Shift+←
Right one cell	Shift+→
Right to the first or last cell of a range	Ctrl+Shift+→
Down one cell	Shift+↓
Up one cell	Shift+↑
Down to the first or last cell of a range	Ctrl+Shift+↓
Up to the first or last cell of a range	Ctrl+Shift+↑
To the beginning of row	Shift+Home
To the end of row	Shift+End
To the beginning of spreadsheet	Ctrl+Shift+Home
To the end of spreadsheet	Ctrl+Shift+End
Up one window	Shift+PgUp
Down one window	Shift+PgDn
Left one window	Ctrl+Shift+PgUp
Right one window	Ctrl+Shift+PgDn
Cancel a selection	Esc

Highlighting in the Database:

To highlight	Press
A record (List) or row (Report)	Ctrl+F8
A field (List) or column (Report)	Shift+F8
An entire database (List or Report)	Ctrl+Shift+F8
Left one field	Shift+←
Right one field	Shift+→
A record, to the first field entry	Ctrl+Shift+←
A record, to the last field entry	Ctrl+Shift+→
Down one field	Shift+↓
Up one field	Shift+↑
A field, down to the last record	Ctrl+Shift+↓
A field, up to the first record	Ctrl+Shift+↑
To the beginning of record	Shift+Home
To the end of record	Shift+End
To the beginning of database	Ctrl+Shift+Home
To the end of database	Ctrl+Shift+End
Up one window (List view)	Shift+PgUp
Down one window (List view)	Shift+PgDn
Left one window (List view)	Ctrl+Shift+PgUp
Right one window (List view)	Ctrl+Shift+PgDn

Editing Keys

Changing Document Information:

To	Press
Copy selection	Ctrl+C
Paste selection	Ctrl+V
Cut selection	Ctrl+X
Delete selection (WP only)	Del or Backspace
Undo changes in the Word Processor	Ctrl+Z
Repeat search	F7
Edit cell	F2
Copy the values of above cell	Ctrl+' (apost.)
Paginate document	F9
Calculate spreadsheet	F9
Go To	F5

Changing Appearance of Text or Cells:

To	*Press*
Make text bold	Ctrl+B
Make text italic	Ctrl+I
Make text subscript	Ctrl+=
Make text superscript	Ctrl+Shift+=
Underline text	Ctrl+U
Remove all font styles	Ctrl+Spacebar
Repeat format	Shift+F7

To change cells/fields to	*Press*
Comma format	Ctrl+, (comma)
Currency format	Ctrl+4
Percent format	Ctrl+5

Inserting Information:

To insert	*Press*
A tab stop	Tab
A new paragraph	Enter
The current date	Ctrl+;
The current time	Ctrl+Shift+;

Word Processor only

A page break	Ctrl+Enter
An optional hyphen	Ctrl+–
A nonbreaking hyphen	Ctrl+Shift+–
A nonbreaking space	Ctrl+Shift+Space

Word Processor and Database form view only

An end-of-line mark	Shift+Enter

Spreadsheet only

Create Autosum total	Ctrl+M

Formatting Paragraphs:

To	*Press*
Single space lines	Ctrl+1
Double space lines	Ctrl+2
Space lines 1.5 lines apart	Ctrl+5
Reduce space before paragraph	Ctrl+0 (zero)
Add space before paragraph	Ctrl+O (letter O)
Centre text	Ctrl+E

156

Justify text	Ctrl+J
Left align text	Ctrl+L
Right align text	Ctrl+R
Remove paragraph styles	Ctrl+Q
Add hanging indent	Ctrl+H
Undo hanging indent	Ctrl+G
Add nested indent	Ctrl+N
Undo nested indent	Ctrl+M

Working in the Formula Bar:

These shortcuts can be used in the formula bar of Database, Reporting, or Spreadsheet tools.

To	*Press*
Activate and clear the formula bar	Backspace or Del
Confirm information in a cell or field	Enter
Confirm information in a range of cells	Ctrl+Enter
Change information in a cell or field	F2

Choosing Menus and Commands:

The <Alt> key pressed with the underlined letter of any menu command will open that menu. Some other shortcuts are:

To	*Press*
Save a document	Ctrl+S
Get Help	F1
Activate the menu bar	F10
Choose the Tutorial	Shift+F1
Choose the Insert menu	Alt+I
Print a document	Ctrl+P
Close any open menu	Esc
Open the Font box on the toolbar	Ctrl+F
Open the Font Size box on the toolbar	Ctrl+K
Switch between form view and list view	F3
Switch between spreadsheet and chart	F3
Toggle absolute cell (Spreadsheet)	F4
Toggle select title text (Charting)	Ctrl+T
Paginate Word Processor document	F9
Calculate spreadsheet	F9
Quit Works	Alt+F4

INDEX

A

Absolute addressing 90
Active
  cell 70
  window 11
Address book 138
Alignment
  box 42
  cell 73, 92
Automatic
  cell fill 92
  column widths 92
Autosum 80
AVG function 81, 147

B

Backspace key 27
Bar chart 96
Bold 25, 156
Borders 44, 72
Bookmark 34
Breakfield 131
Buttons/icons 24

C

Caret (^) character 56
Cell
  address 69
  alignment 92
  formatting ... 77, 93, 115
Centre
  across columns 129
  tabs 50
  justify 37
Change
  active window 10
  drive/directory 19

Character enhancement 36
Chart 94
  Editor 98
  font and size 102
  grid lines 103
  save 100
  titles 102
Check
  box 9
  spelling 57
Clear cells 81
Closing a window 15
Column
  automatic widths 92
  insert 87
  widths 74, 88, 111
Command button 9
Communications 137
Control
  box 11
  panel 22
Copy
  cells 80
  text 31
Copyright 2
Count (words) 59
Create
  drawing 67
  new file 14, 69
  report 124
Cue Cards 13
Currency format 74
Custom tabs 50
Cut (text) 31

D

Data-files 107

Database
  create 108
  editing 112
  entry form 110
  field 107
  FIND command 120
  form view 108, 110
  formulae 114
  list view 108
  printing 123
  query 107, 120
  record 107
  report 124
  screens 108
  searching 120
  sorting 116
  statistical operators . 130
  Toolbar 122
Date
  arithmetic 116
  codes in WP 53
  current 119
  format 116
  formulae 36
  functions 117, 149
  number 117
  reset 119
Date and time functions   149
Decimal tabs 50
Defining a report 128
Delete key 29
Deleting
  cells (Clear) 81
  text 29, 32
Dialogue box 8
Document editing 29
Double spaced text   43, 156
Draft
  printing 47
  view 35
Drag and Drop 31

Draw tool 63

E
Edit
  Clear command 81
  Copy command ... 31, 80
  Cut command 31
  document 29
  drawing 68
  entry form 112
  Fill Down command .. 80
  Paste command .. 31, 80
  Undo command ... 33, 93
Editing keys 155
End mark 27
Enhancement
  character 36
  text 50
Enter button 72
Entering
  data 71, 78, 113
  text 27
Erase data 81
Exiting Works 21, 77
Exploded pie chart 104
EXT message 30

F
F1 key (Help) 7
F2 key (Edit) 72, 77, 90
F5 key (Go To) 34, 71
F8 key (Select) 30, 129
F9 key
  (Calculate) 82
  (Database view) 109
  (Paginate) 34
F10 key (View) 82
Field in database 107
File
  Exit command 21, 77
  extensions 15

management 18
open 20, 77
Print 47, 83
retrieve 20, 77
Save As 19
Save 18, 75
types 20
Fill Down 80
Financial functions 145
Find
  text 55
  command 120
Fonts 38, 73
Footer margin 48
Footers 51
Footnotes 51
Form 110
  letters 134
  screen 110
Format commands
  Autoformat 93
  Border 72
  colours 93
  currency 74
  font 38, 73
  patterns 93
  tab settings 50
  Time/Date 116
Formula bar 70, 157
Formulae 78, 114, 130
Freehand drawing 67
Freezing titles 88
Function Insert 93
Functions 79, 132
  Date and Time 149
  Financial 145
  Logical 145
  Mathematical 144
  Special 149
  Statistical 147
  Text 147

G
Gallery command 98
Go To command 34, 71
Graph types 95
Graphic insert 62

H
Hanging indents 43
Hard disc 1
Headers 51
Header margins 48
Help 7, 110, 137
Hide (field) 113
Highlighting keystrokes
  Database 155
  Spreadsheet 154
  Word processor 153
Home key 70

I
Icons 24
IF function 118, 145
Indenting text 42
Insert
  blank line 29
  columns/rows 87
  function 93, 143
  mode 29
  note 59
  picture 62
Installing Works 1
Integrated package ... 1, 23
Italics 25, 38, 156

J
Justification 37, 42

L
Layered drawings 68
Learning (Tutorials) 21

Left
  justify 37, 42
  tabs 50
Line chart 95, 99
Line drawing 68
List
  box 9
  screen 107, 109
Locking fields 115
Logical functions 145

M

Mail merge 134
Main menu 5
Managing files 18
Manipulating windows ... 13
Manual page break mark 33
Mathematical functions . 144
Maximise
  button 16
  window 16
Menu bar 5
Microsoft Draw 63
Minimise box 12
Mixed chart types 105
Mouse operation 9, 24
Moving
  around database 152
  around dialogue box 151
  around document 27, 151
  around form 114
  around spreadsheet 152
  text 31
  window 15
Multiple windows 13

N

Navigation 34, 70, 151
Nested indents 43
New (file) 4

Non-breaking
  hyphen 156
  space 156
Non-contiguous range .. 90
Normal view 35
Notes 59

O

OLE (Object linking) 63
On-line help 7
On-line tutorial 21
Open file 20
Option box 8
Overstrike mode 29

P

Page
  break 33
  length 48
  margin 48
  mark 33
  numbers 52
  Setup 48
  titles 130
  width 48
Page Layout view 35
Paginate 34
Paper size 48
Paragraph
  borders 44
  definition 41
  format 41, 156
  headers 51
  mark 41
Paste command 31, 90
Paste Special command 97
Pattern fill 93
Picture
  box 62
  insert 64
Pie chart 104

162

Point size 39
Preview 35, 83, 133
Print
    area 84
    chart 103
    database 123
    document 45
    form letters 136
    from a file 47
    Preview 35, 83, 133
    report 133
    spreadsheet 83
Printer port 45
Printer set-up 45
Protect data 115

Q
Query 120, 133
Quick key comb's 28, 82, 151
Quit program 21, 77

R
Radar chart type 96
Record 107
Reference marks 56
Relative addressing 90
Repagination 34
Replacing text 32, 55
Report
    create 124
    definition 128
    icon 126
    formulae 130
    name 129
    print 133
    query 133
    row types 127
    sort 131
    title 129
Restore buttons 12
Retrieving a file 20

Right
    justify 37, 42
    tabs 50
Row 69
    insert 87
Ruler 26, 44

S
Sample files 141
Save
    As 19
    charts 100
    file 18
    worksheet 75
    workspace 8
Scroll
    bar 12
    box 11
Search
    criteria 120
    database 120
    for text 55
Select All 84
Selected cell 11
Selecting text 29
Set date & time 119
Setting print area 84
Settings (Options) 8
Setup program 1
Shading cells 93
Show
    all characters 41
    ruler 26
Single spaced text . 43, 156
Sort
    database 116
    report 131
Special
    codes 53
    characters 37, 56
    functions 149

Spell checker 57
Split bar 11, 17
Spreadsheet
    alignment 73
    Autosum 80
    cell addressing 90
    Charts 94
    editing 77
    formulae 78
    functions 79
    labels 72
    open/retrieve 77
    print 83
    Quick keys 82
    ranges 90
    save 75
    Toolbar 85
    UNDO command 93
Stacked line chart 95
Standard headers 51
Starting program 3
Statistical
    functions 147
    operators 130
Status bar 13
SUM function 79, 147
Synonym 58

T
Tab
    leaders 51
    settings 50
Templates 139
Text
    box 9
    copy 31
    delete 32
    emboldening 38
    enhancement 37, 50
    functions 147
    justification 37, 42

move 31
replace 32
select 29
underline 25, 37
Thesaurus 58
Tile windows 18
Time format 149
Title
    bar 12
    freeze 88
    report 129
Toolbar 12
    charting 95
    customise 25
    database 122
    draw 65
    spreadsheet 85
    word processor 24
Tutorial 21
Two Y-axes 106
Type of file 20

U
Underline 25, 37
UNDO command 33, 93

V
View commands 35

W
WCM extension 15
WDB extension 15, 108
Welcome screen 4
White space 56
Widths, automatic 92
Window
    active 15
    arrange 13
    close 15
    maximise 16

move 15
size 16
split 17
WKS extension 15, 76
Word processor 23
WordArt 61
Word
   count 59
   meaning 58
   wrap 27
Works
   database 107
   draw 63
   exiting 21, 77
   install 1
   graphs/charts 94
   sample files 141

screen 10
settings 9
spreadsheet 69
starting 3
templates 139
tutorial 21
Wizards 5, 137
word processor 23
Worksheet charts 94
WorksWizards 137
WPS extension 15, 24

X
X-Y chart 96

Z
Zoom views 35

NOTES

NOTES

NOTES

NOTES

NOTES

NOTES

NOTES